DAVID C SMITH
C297 PENNINGTON
FURNESS COLLEGE
LANCASTER UNIVERSITY
LANCASTER

Accounting Principles and the City Code:
The Case for Reform

Accounting Principles and the City Code:
The Case for Reform

by

EDWARD STAMP

(Professor of Accounting and Business Method in the University of Edinburgh)

and

CHRISTOPHER MARLEY

(Financial Editor of *The Times*)

Butterworths
1970

ENGLAND:	BUTTERWORTH & CO. (PUBLISHERS) LTD. LONDON: 88 Kingsway, W.C.2
AUSTRALIA:	BUTTERWORTH & CO. (AUSTRALIA) LTD. SYDNEY: 20 Loftus Street MELBOURNE: 343 Little Collins Street BRISBANE: 240 Queen Street
CANADA:	BUTTERWORTH & CO. (CANADA) LTD. TORONTO: 14 Curity Avenue, 374
NEW ZEALAND:	BUTTERWORTH & CO. (NEW ZEALAND) LTD. WELLINGTON: 49/51 Ballance Street AUCKLAND: 35 High Street
SOUTH AFRICA:	BUTTERWORTH & CO. (SOUTH AFRICA) LTD. DURBAN: 33/35 Beach Grove

©
Edward Stamp and Christopher Marley
1970

ISBN: 0 406 49120 8

Made and printed in Great Britain
at the St Ann's Press, Park Road, Altrincham

Contents

Preface ix

Part One: The City Code (Christopher Marley)

1 **First Attempts at Guidance** 3
    The unrestricted stock-market 3
    Post-war equity boom 4
    The City at loggerheads 6
    First notes on amalgamations 8

2 **Provocation 1966-67** 11
    The Pye Consortium 12
    Courtaulds and the textile wholesalers 14
    Metal Industries won and lost 16

3 **The 1968 City Code** 20
    Drafting of the Code 20
    Rules and principles 21

4 **The Panel on Trial** 25
    Courtaulds, Dufay, and International Paints ... 25
    The Panel tries censure 29
    American fight for Gallaher 29
    City argument with the Panel 32

5 **Demise of the Old Panel** 35
    Toning down a censure 35
    Expansion of Pergamon Press 36
    News of the World and Pergamon 37
    Proposals for a new Panel 40

6 **The 1969 City Code** 42
    New Panel staff 42
    Penalties for breaking the rules 43
    New rules of conduct 44

7	**New Panel's Test of Strength**	48
	Pergamon agreement with Leasco	48
	Leasco's anxieties	50
	Collapse of the merger	51
	Findings of the Panel	54
8	**The Scope of Regulation**	57
	Achievements and failures	57
	Operational philosophy	58
	The widening net of supervision	59
	The weakness of divided authority	61

Part Two: Reforming Accounting Principles (Edward Stamp)

9	**A Crisis in the Accounting Profession**	65
	Criticism in America	66
	Criticism in Britain	68
	English Institute under fire	72
10	**Accounting Principles: The Challenge**	74
	The nature of financial accounts	74
	The inutility of British accounts	76
	'Stewardship' accounting	77
	Accounting principles: the conventional wisdom	78
	The proliferation of new rules and procedures	82
	Some specific problems	84
	Goodwill	85
	Revenue from Long-term contracts	86
	Leaseholds	87
	Discount on debentures	88
	The distinction between profits and retained profits	88
	A plethora of 'principles'	90
	Research by the Scottish Institute	92
	A clear need for reform	95
11	**Accounting Principles: The American Response**	97
	British accountancy lacking in vigour?	97
	First American steps: the SEC	100
	Formation of Committee on Accounting Procedure	102
	The Accounting Principles Board	104

12	**Accounting Principles: The British Response**	109
	A suggestion to the English Institute	110
	British academic accounting	113
	British progress to date	114
	The apathy of British accountants	117
13	**'The True and Fair View'—The Ambiguous Position of the Auditor**	119
	Who is the auditor's client?	119
	Some difficulties for the auditor	122
	The auditor as a Judge	123
14	**Uniformity or Flexibility: The False Dichotomy**	129
	The utility of financial accounts	129
	A plethora of methods	130
	Management's attitudes to the future	132
	Consistency: a tool, not a principle	133
	The need for comparability	135
	Some pitfalls to avoid	138
15	**Proposals for Reform**	141
	What is needed	141
	Who should solve the problem	143
	Parliament and the profession	143
	A British SEC	143
	Management	144
	The profession	145
	The English Institute's plans	145
	The approach of the scientist	147
	A programme for the profession	148
	Definition of objectives	148
	Terminology	148
	Data collection on current practice	149
	Independence of the auditor	149
	The problem of 'teeth'	150
	Full disclosure	150
	An Accounting Principles Board	151
	An Accounting Court	152
	A Research Foundation	152
	Fees	153
	Academic participation	153

Appendices

I	(a) Article by Professor Stamp. *The Times*, 11 September 1969	155
	(b) Reply by Mr. Leach. *The Times*, 22 September 1969	160
	(c) Letter to *The Times* from Professor Stamp, 26 September 1969	165
II	*Accountancy*, and a 'true and fair view'	166
III	'The Public Accountant and the Public Interest', from *The Journal of Business Finance*, Vol. 1, No. 1.	168
IV	The City Code on Take-overs and Mergers ...	188

Preface

The authors will always be amongst the first to applaud evidence of British financial acumen and expertise. Along with scientific and technological skill, it forms the bedrock upon which this country's future economic viability rests, and the springboard from which new thrusts can be made. Why then have we chosen to write a book so critical of those twin pillars of the British financial establishment, the City and the accounting profession?

The reasons are quite simple. We believe that recent events confirm our judgement that the needs of investors are not being adequately served at the present time. It is our view that, whilst the problems are widely recognised, their true nature has not been properly analysed and diagnosed and, accordingly, no one has yet developed a comprehensive plan for their solution. Planning solutions to problems is perhaps an approach which finds more favour in America than in Britain. The British are supposed to prefer to 'muddle through'. As a number of hostile armies have discovered to their cost, the British approach can be supremely successful. But we believe that it is not appropriate to the solution of the difficulties which confront this country today—particularly in the economic sphere.

Thus, we have made an attempt to diagnose some of the problems confronting the City and the accounting profession, and to prescribe what we believe to be constructive solutions to these problems. We do not pretend to have covered them all, and we would be foolish if we thought we were offering a panacea. But we hope what we have to say will be helpful.

A brief word as to the immediate provenance of the book, and its format, is in order. The original idea for the book came from Butterworths who, having read Edward Stamp's article in *The Times* on 11 September 1969 (*see* Appendix I), asked him if he would be interested in working the ideas through in a book. Professor Stamp proposed that the book should also deal with the City Code, and suggested a joint venture with Christopher Marley.

PREFACE

In this way we have been able to bring together two quite different aspects of a general problem: how can the needs of British investors be better served?

Part I of the book, written by Christopher Marley, deals with the City Code and the City Panel, their history and development, and proposals for their future. Part II, written by Edward Stamp, deals with accounting principles and their deficiencies, and suggests a programme for reform. Although we have each read the other's work in manuscript, neither of us pretends to be an expert in the other's field and our writing has therefore employed the pronoun 'I', where necessary, rather than 'we'. (Neither of us finds the use of the 'Royal' 'we' acceptable!)

We are grateful to *The Times* for permission to reproduce the material in Appendix I (which was first published in *The Times*); and to Business Publications Ltd., publishers of *The Journal of Business Finance,* and Professor J. R. Perrin (Editor of that journal) for permission to reproduce (as Appendix III) the article 'The Public Accountant and the Public Interest' which was first published in Vol. 1, No. 1, of *The Journal of Business Finance.* The Issuing Houses Association has kindly allowed us to print the City Code on Take-overs and Mergers in Appendix IV. Christopher Marley would also like to acknowledge the help and assistance of many people in the City, and the permission of Mr. William Rees-Mogg, Editor of *The Times,* to write this book.

Edward Stamp
Christopher Marley

Edinburgh
7 January 1970

Part One

The City Code

by
Christopher Marley

1

First Attempts at Guidance

'It is for a shareholder to decide for himself whether to sell or retain his shares.' *Notes on Amalgamations of British Businesses,* the City Working Party, October 1959.

The Unrestricted Stock-Market

The unity of the City of London is the staple of caricature. The City can take its contribution to public welfare with a seriousness that invites hostility. From collective attitudes on the respectability of its function and the respectability with which it is carried out, there is only a short step to the still frequently voiced opinion that interference in the City's activities is not merely presumptuous but positively harmful to the nation at large. The City would argue that it cannot fulfill its proper mission if closely regulated.

Somewhere along the line this variegated community's elders omit the fact that the job of all institutions which make up the golden square mile at the centre of the capitalist system is to make money. They make it. Almost as easily forgotten is the fact that the City has survived two world wars and a more recent social revolution virtually unregulated.

In its new, architecturally anonymous garb, the Stock Exchange towers above the City. To those even remotely familiar with the scandals, depression and Roosevelt revolution of pre-war American finance, it would come as a shock to see how gradually the London Stock Exchange has moved from *laissez faire* to the minimum of control of the securities markets. No control whatever over the securities dealt in on the Stock Exchange was exercised until well after the First World War: the only matter for concern was whether a stock could be turned over. In the middle of the 1960s as he moved up to retirement, Mr. Esmond Durlacher, senior partner of London's largest and best-known jobbers or wholesalers of shares, used to look back fondly to the pre-war days when he could be a real *market* man, turning over the whole capital of a company in a day. Those were indeed the days for a shrewd dealer. Even when the Exchange took its first step in 1921 to supervise the conduct of the market, the only restriction on what was actually dealt in was that the Exchange technically had to approve. The worldwide events of the late 1920s, and more particularly the legendary collapse in Britain of Clarence Hatry's financial empire, forced the Exchange General Purposes Committee into a momentous decision of principle—that any new issue to be dealt in on the London market had to be investigated to see that adequate information had been made available to investors (and that 'persons whose standing and repute were known to be in question' had nothing to do with the company).

It has been the Stock Exchange boast ever since that it has always required greater disclosure from company management than the law demands. Despite the monumental advances in information provided in accordance with two post-war Companies Acts, and despite the influence of the much neglected Jenkins Committee on company law reform, the point about City institutions is that their members' professional conduct is subject to the rules of their own professional clubs—in essence the City answers to itself for its own behaviour. That is fact, not judgement. The question for judgement is whether self-discipline has meant inadequate discipline. In one area at least the City's evolution from *laissez faire* can be examined in detail. That, of course, is in its most public activity, the conduct of take-over bids. The attempt to win control of a publicly known enterprise has exhibited the financier to lay observers of the business scene in a context they can readily understand. For the City, the exploitation and progress of bids and mergers since the war has brought a concentration of public opinion on its operations in general. It is fair to say that that exposure has done more than anything else to change the City's methods of operation. It is still doing so.

Post-War Equity Boom

Two simple factors combined to get the merger boom under way. The first, the realisation that inflation was to be part of the way of life. With that realisation the cult of the equity was born.

FIRST ATTEMPTS AT GUIDANCE

Only the ordinary shares of a company bear the real risks and the real rewards of capitalism. Provided the fixed sums of interest and fixed dividends of other classes of capital can be paid, ordinary shares are entitled to the rest of the profits. The age of decline in the purchasing power of money, of rising prices and rising profits, led to a massive investment shift into ordinary shares, gradual but constant.

The second was that the free market was subjected to its first real taste of national control. The power of companies to pay out their profits to shareholders as dividends was heavily restricted. There were two obvious results. First, companies began to accumulate cash; but since dividends were still the arbiter of the value of a company's shares in the stock-market, share prices were often artificially low and the capital value of the enterprise in stock-market terms small. Secondly, with inflation the monetary value of productive assets like land, buildings and machinery was rising, in many cases at a rate faster than that of the decline in the purchasing power of money. Property was the most significant case. Companies which had bought factories and office buildings decades earlier carried them in their accounts at cost or written down value, often blithely unaware of the dramatic prices they would realise if put up for sale in the post-war market. It was a situation that invited the attentions of the financially shrewd, particularly those with some knowledge or ability in real estate.

Throughout the 1950s the process gathered pace. Once demonstrated, it was a simple enough technique to make what looked like a generous bid for a company's shares; and then, when in control, to sell the property to, and lease it back from, an insurance company anxious to counter inflation itself by investing in real estate; the proceeds and the acquired company's own cash could then be mobilised for the next deal and so on to the multi-millions. It was the age symbolised by the public awareness of Mr. Charles Clore, who had graduated from an ice rink in Cricklewood to a series of gigantic investments in property, shoe shops, stores, car distribution, engineering or any good, under-utilised asset.

It was the age when the public got a distorted picture of the bidder as a man prepared to fight a battle over stocks and shares from which he would emerge richer and richer, somehow depriving the innocent or the naïve of their rightful inheritance.

As the targets for bids became larger and more important, emotionally charged conflicts superseded old-fashioned, agreed unions. Mr. Clore himself was simply rebuffed when he tried to absorb the great brewing chain of Watney Mann, and he was quite unable to make any headway at all.

The City at Loggerheads

Behind the contestants, the entrepreneurs and the professional and traditional managers, stood the City, the merchant bankers and the stockbrokers. The whole operation of the City was, and stilll is, based on confidence between honourable men. They provided the finance or the market expertise—how to get to the nation's shareholders in the most persuasive and the cheapest way, whether the shareholders were private individuals or sophisticated institutions. The City developed its own front-line fighting expertise and charged for it on the basis of the value of a merger transaction. The percentage might be small, but the bigger the bids became, the more money was at stake for the merchant bankers. It is a tribute to a vanishing financial class system that it took so long for anyone to scream 'foul' loudly. When the scream did come, it was multi-voiced and very loud. Fittingly, the occasion had the elements of a good romantic melodrama. Not only did the battle for British Aluminium represent a major confrontation between the old and the new in merchant banking itself. It was also basically a fight between two American companies for a British one, allowing patriotism as well as money and financial propriety to embitter the argument.

The British Aluminium affair is too well known to be raked over in detail. The company, with a one-third share of the market in a fast growing industry, was a classic 'situation'—profits were falling, the share price had halved in a year or two and money was needed to expand. That, and the existence of a useful new plant in Canada, attracted the attention of Reynolds Metals of the United States. Reynolds was advised in New York to go into partnership with a British company to acquire British Aluminium, thereby to forestall the forces of economic nationalism. Reynolds was also advised to use the services of merchant bankers, S. G. Warburg. That was in 1957. Only eleven years earlier Mr. Siegmund Warburg had founded his London merchant bank—though a member of a famous European banking family, he had left Germany for Britain

FIRST ATTEMPTS AT GUIDANCE

in 1934—and it was in 1957 that, by a union with Seligman Brothers, S. G. Warburg had become a member of the Accepting Houses Committee, the hallmark of an established merchant banking house. Warburg had the credentials, but the British Aluminium battle made his reputation. Reynolds went into partnership with one of Britain's largest engineering groups, Tube Investments. Tube Investments in turn was advised by two merchant banks, themselves later to join forces, Schroders and Helbert Wagg.

The Reynolds camp began buying shares in British Aluminium under the traditional cover of nominee names and by the autumn of 1958, when the cards started coming out on the table, the holding had been built up to 10 per cent of the capital. Viscount Portal, of RAF fame, and Mr. Geoffrey Cunliffe, respectively chairman and managing director of British Aluminium, knew the buying was under way, but not its source. If there had to be a union with anybody, they and their joint advisers, the esteemed banking houses of Hambros and Lazards, had their own candidate. That was Alcoa, the Aluminium company of America.

Early in November 1958 Sir Ivan Steddeford of Tube Investments tried to open negotiations with Lord Portal of British Aluminium and then attempted a definite offer. He was rebuffed, came out into the open with a take-over bid and made it clear that BA would remain in British control with Tube Investments holding 51 and Reynolds 49 per cent of the capital.

That the bid was rejected out of hand brought criticism enough. But within weeks British Aluminium announced a deal with Alcoa whereby it would issue enough new shares in the company—with no need to consult its own shareholders—to give Alcoa a one-third interest and effectively to block the Reynolds–Tube Investments bid. To the incredulity of observers this arrangement was argued to be American collaboration not American domination. Tempers rose quickly in the City. Behind British Aluminium, Lazards and Hambros ranged a galaxy of famous merchant banks into a consortium which made a rival offer for the company; and Lord Kindersley and Mr. Olaf Hambro, chairmen of the two leading banks, urged British Aluminium's shareholders that the Reynolds offer should be resisted in the national interest. It was the voice of authority but to shareholders it was also the voice of reaction. The shareholding institutions of the City, the trusts and the insurance companies, were appalled by such an argument and dumped their shares in the stock-market. There the Warburg–Reynolds–Tube Investments axis were well organised for a hectic buying spree which took them to a massive victory over a crumpled but hostile merchant banking establishment.

The bitterness and the division ran deep. The network of gentility and politeness broke down completely; far from keeping in touch with each other, the opposing merchant banks indulged in personal animosity and their partners literally crossed the road to avoid each other. The worst aspect of the matter of course was that the public had had a ringside seat to observe that, when it came down to ethics and propriety, the top figures of the City, far from being in agreement, were at each other's throats. British Aluminium was not the only problem. However, it raised the major questions of City practice and, though preceded in the summer of 1958 by a three-cornered tussle over Harrods and followed immediately in the summer of 1959 by Mr. Clore's abortive attempt to enter the brewing industry by acquiring Watneys, it still remained the *cause célèbre* of the decade. That demanded action. The City's acknowledged leader, the Governor of the Bank of England, called together a working party of his satellites, the executive committee of the Issuing Houses Association in co-operation with the Accepting Houses Committee (effectively the merchant banks), the Association of Investment Trusts, the British Insurance Association, the Committee of London Clearing Bankers (the big five conventional banks), and the Stock Exchange. Between them they produced *Notes on Amalgamations of British Businesses*.

First Notes on Amalgamations

It was not that rules of behaviour had to be devised for the City itself. The working party summed the matter up as only a committee can.

The original *Notes* were issued because these organisations felt that it would be useful to draw up a general guide to the principles and practices which should be followed by those concerned in transactions which have as their object the transfer of the control of a company out of the hands of existing shareholders into new hands. Most transactions of this type take place without controversy, but because some inevitably are carried out in the face of opposition in one form or another it is important that the principles and practices followed in them should be under continuous examination and development.

The *Notes*, with a subsequent revision, entitled shareholders to natural justice. The principles were vague ('Boards of directors must at all times bear in mind the interests of all the holders of all the respective classes of share and loan capital of their companies, according to their respective rights'). The procedural recommendations were no more pointed ('The board of the offeree company should decide as rapidly as possible its attitude to situations as they develop, and should inform shareholders of it'.)

And regulation remained a long way off. Far from there being any suggestion of supervising how people conducted themselves in the stock-market during the course of a take-over bid, the first principle of the *Notes* enshrined the belief that 'there should be no interference with the free market in shares and securities of companies.'

Nevertheless, British Aluminium was a turning point in the postwar development of the City. Without doubt, for example, it brought a new sense of professionalism into merchant banking; and once there was a commitment on methodology, however vague, there was no going back. In fact, an almost forgotten imbroglio of 1963 called for an important revision of the working party's notes. That was a bid by the state-owned Richard Thomas & Baldwins steel company (the only major steel enterprise not to have been denationalised by the Tories) for the stock-market quoted Whitehead Iron & Steel. RTB ran into opposition from one of the denationalised giants, Stewarts & Lloyds; but, advised by Rothschilds, the state-owned group virtually ensured the success of its bid by agreeing to purchase the shareholdings of the big institutions in the stock-market, at the same time undertaking to pay the institutions the difference between the then market price of their shares and any higher bid that RTB might make.

The institutions could not lose and they accepted those generous terms. Private shareholders, however, with less individual or cumulative power, were left to their own unfortunate devices and not offered the same deal. In its day Whitehead Iron was considered a minor sensation and the City working party was reconvened to publish a new version of the Queensberry rules, *Revised Notes on Company Amalgamations and Mergers*. There was no indiscreet reference to recent conduct. With a passing observation to the Board of Trade's 1960 introduction of the Licensed Dealers (Conduct of

Business) Rules and of the report of the Jenkins Committee on company law reform, the new document blandly observed that 'The organisations concerned in the preparation of the original *Notes* feel that the time has now come to modify them.'

The major modification centred on stock-market dealings in the course of a take-over bid. A bidder who published his terms, the procedural rules declared, 'and who subsequently acquires effective control by buying, in the market or otherwise, should without delay revise his existing offer or make a formal offer to all uncommitted shareholders at a fair price having regard to the prices made in the market. Purchases of some of the shares of any particular class, whether made through the market or otherwise, should not be made with special conditions attached which are not available to all shareholders of that class.'

Taken together with the Stock Exchange's own *General Undertaking,* which effectively banned the British Aluminium potential manoeuvre of issuing unissued shares to a favoured suitor, the City seemed to have established a simple principle—that all shareholders had equal rights in a take-over bid and were not to be misled by the directors or in the market place into a worse deal than some other more powerful shareholder.

2

Provocation 1966-67

'To suggest that an intention seven years ago is binding is to do the English language an injustice.' John Gillum, director Kleinwort Benson.

When Mr. Harold Wilson's Labour government scraped into power at the end of 1964 it mustered an unpredictable group of supporters. Neither the City nor industry could ever be described as enthusiasts for an avowedly socialist Prime Minister. But the fever chart of the economy had certainly been a trial for both. The bull market on the Stock Exchange moved to a climax after the election victory and both in the City and industry there was a warm welcome for the government's increasingly voiced demands for a new industrial revolution. The economics of scale needed to meet international competition, and the restructuring of British industry, became the catch phrases of the financial establishment. Mergers, consistently vilified in the past as the technique of the unscrupulous entrepreneur, became positively respectable. There was a snag, of course. The balance of payments was a nightmare, inherited or not, and freeze and squeeze were the order of the day.

The stock-market went into sharp decline with a general collapse of share prices which continued through 1965 and 1966. Though by no means obvious at the time, the nadir was reached at the end of 1966; it was not a good time for confidence, on which the take-over business naturally thrives. But the mood of the market changed dramatically from the beginning of 1967. It was not that the economy was coming right; but national and international upheaval, a spiral in interest rates, and the growing prospect of devaluation caused a real flight from money of dubious value. The one place to fly was ordinary shares and a boom born of lack of confidence got under way. From early 1967 to January 1969 it was almost possible to shut your eyes and be sure of a capital gain on the London stock-market. That was just the right time for putting take-over bids through. Target companies, valued in line with their last published profits which reflected the worst of the squeeze, might be bought relatively cheaply just when there was the possibility that the worst was over. There were other factors too.

The Pye Consortium

Trouble is the shrewd buyer's opportunity. Nearly forty years earlier, for instance, an Irishman, C. O. Stanley, had the opportunity to buy a small radio firm called Pye for £60,000. He offered it to the Dutch group Philips for £65,000, but Philips baulked at that extra £5,000. Stanley kept Pye and built it up into a nationally known radio, television and electronics group. But despite Stanley's record and his enthusiasm —he did not restrain himself from telling the market what his share price should be—in 1966 Pye was overstretched and in trouble. Philips had already reappeared on the scene and bought 5 per cent of the Pye equity as a prelude to a deal with C. O. Stanley and his son. But meanwhile Pye's misfortunes had led to a stand-up boardroom row and the Stanleys were eased out of executive office in the company.

In the London market stockbroker Mr. Edgar Astaire, head of his own firm, Astaire & Co., regarded a situation like Pye as the name of the financial game. He started to acquire shares with the object of presenting a potential bidder for the company with a strategic holding and of making himself a good profit in the process. Astaire had gone to New York investment bankers Burnham & Co. with his own ideas of which American company might do well to buy Pye. Among Burnham's clients was the Dutch Philips.

Towards the close of November 1966 Philips announced a take-over bid for Pye of 8s. a share or nearly £20m. In London Edgar Astaire continued buying and the Pye share price began to move comfortably ahead of the value of the Philips bid. Pye, however, attracted the attentions of another bidder, Sir Jules Thorn's Thorn Electrical Industries. Thorn had built his empire from a pre-war trade in light bulbs into the country's dominant radio and television group and into one of the stock-market's darling companies with a proved ability to keep profits growing consistently. Anxious to move into Pye's telecommunications business, Thorn countered Philips by offering 10s. 9d. a share for Pye in mid-

December, but the Pye share price moved above that figure. In the market the Astaire consortium was still hard at work.

Questions began to be asked. After all, the *Revised Notes on Mergers* said that a bidder who bought control in the stockmarket should without delay revise his existing offer. If Philips were buying Pye shares at 10s., having made an offer of 8s. a share, someone had the right to be upset—particularly when Philips finally unveiled a new bid of £30m. or 12s. a share. Philips was specific that it was not buying in the market.

Shortly after the Thorn bid, Edgar Astaire widened his buying consortium with the inclusion of a top firm of stock brokers, Scrimgeours, and the shares came flooding in at prices up to 12s. A couple of days before Christmas Philips announced both its 12s. bid and the fact that it had, that day, bought 19 per cent of Pye's ordinary shares. It was a knock-out blow—with a total of 24 per cent of the capital and a 12s. bid Philips was unassailable.

There was no disguising the fact that the sellers were the Astaire-Scrimgeours consortium, with a major role played by Burnham & Co. of New York. Who instructed Burnham? Philips was explicit about who did not: 'N. V. Philips further confirmed to Philips Industries that at no time before the 23rd (of December) had it, or any of its subsidiaries, been beneficially interested directly or indirectly in the shares now purchased.' The London Stock Exchange, whose memorandum of guidance on bids precluded the use of the market 'as a cloak for dealing covertly in a manner inconsistent with public statements' accepted that neither Thorn nor Philips were responsible for the buying. The *Sunday Times* in London asked for an enquiry. That paper's New York correspondent spoke to a Burnham & Co. partner, Andries D. Woudhuysen who was described as saying 'There was nothing mysterious about the transactions. From the very beginning we acted under sole instructions of and on behalf of Philips. We went out into the market and bought shares on behalf of a client.' A day later Woudhuysen retracted that statement—Philips was not the client. In theory at least Philips was right. In London Edgar Astaire, while not disclaiming the point of the market operation, still argues that the rules were not broken. 'The consortium never had a contract with Philips. If Philips had withdrawn from the affair we would have carried the loss. It was our responsibility.'

In theory there the matter rested. But there was no denying that the spirit of the Queensberry rules should have deterred a covert market operation of this sort even if the letter did not; while the City debated and asked for explanations, positive action was conspicuous by its absence.

Courtaulds and the Textile Wholesalers

Sir Jules Thorn did not forget the fact. But before he could reappear on the take-over scene another industrial knight began to make the City headlines. Sir Frank Kearton,[1] chairman of the textile giant Courtaulds, owed his ultimate power to the most famous take-over attempt of all, the bid by the largest industrial enterprise in the country, Imperial Chemical Industries, to buy Courtaulds in 1961. Perhaps the major ploy in Courtaulds' successful defence was to bring its professional managers, and Kearton in particular, to the top of the company.

Since 1961 Kearton had guided Courtaulds through a series of vertical and horizontal mergers in the textile industry and by 1967 had decided on mopping up the wholesaling section of the trade. After a series of small but bitter encounters in a period of little more than a year, Kearton, an intellectual of industry and chairman (1966-69) of the Industrial Reorganisation Corporation sponsored by the government, was to launch a controversial attack on the citadels of finance, the merchant banks, the insurance companies and the accounting profession, whose reverberations are still being felt.

It is true to say, however, that he created some trouble himself, by seizing control of textile wholesalers Cook & Watts with a determination that paid scant attention to take-over conventions. Cook & Watts received a take-over bid, which it flatly rejected, from another wholesaler, Macanie, early in 1967. Instead the board unveiled a deal with Courtaulds. Courtaulds sold one of its own subsidiaries to Cook & Watts in exchange for 28 per cent of C & W's shares and, with a proper regard for the competitive ability of the counter-bidder and for the conventions, offered to buy more shares in C & W at the price Macanie had bid. Macanie, backed by one of the City's relatively new men, John Gommes and his bank P. P. Rodoconachi, countered with a higher bid and Courtaulds upped its buying price in the stock-market to follow suit. The gloves were

---

[1] Sir Frank was made a life peer in the 1970 New Year's Honours List.

off and as soon as Courtaulds acquired bare control in the market, it pulled the plug—there was no more buying of Cook & Watts shares and no general offer to shareholders. The C & W share price plunged, Macanie–Rodoconachi were effectively locked in to their investment as minority shareholders nursing a large paper loss. It was not a combination of tactics to win friends and influence people.

Two weeks later Kearton and Courtaulds bid for another wholesaler, Wilkinson & Riddell, supported again by the board of the target company. The price was to be 11s. 6d. a share. But undeterred by the deliberate frustration of his bid for Cook & Watts, John Gommes entered the lists with an offer of 13s. 3d. a share and an agreement to pass control of Wilkinson & Riddell on to Macanie if he won. A public auction, laughable but orderly, followed with Gommes and Kearton outbidding each other in a series of 3d. and 6d. increases. One of those affected by Courtaulds' assault on Cook & Watts was the small merchant bank of Keyser Ullman. Keysers organised a small group of banks and institutional shareholders pledged to Gommes' support and promised the highest bid of the day. When the formal bidding for Wilkinson & Riddell reached 15s. 3d. a share, Kearton lost his patience, closed his official takeover offer with only 29 per cent acceptance and plunged into the stock-market. Gommes went buying too. On a Tuesday in the fourth week of June 1967 the Wilkinson & Riddell share price shot to 20s., but neither side was home and dry. On the Wednesday attention was switched to the Birmingham Stock Exchange where battle raged for the remaining few shares. The price in Birmingham soared to an incredible 65s. a share, making the humdrum Wilkinson & Riddell a gold mine for the lucky few who had been offered 11s. 6d. a share a few weeks earlier.

That evening the Macanie-Gommes team claimed victory and when their offer closed in July 1967 they had 51.8 per cent of the shares costing more than £1¼m. in total—an average of 17s. 6d. a share. Still fighting, Kearton lodged an official complaint with the Stock Exchange on dealing tactics and challenged the share count. A month later he solved the whole problem by an agreed bid for Macanie and closed the episode. Once again, however, nobody's reputation had been enhanced.

Metal Industries Won and Lost

The Wilkinson & Riddell spectacle had provoked a new wave of criticism just as a larger and equally acrimonious fight was boiling up to a climax. The subject was Metal Industries, which favoured a merger with Thorn Electrical Industries (the loser in the Pye affair a few months earlier). MI, advised by bankers Kleinwort Benson, and Thorn, advised by Hambros, were not allowed to have a peaceful marriage, though they said they had been discussing the union for more than a year.

However, Aberdare Holdings, advised by bankers Robert Fleming, courted MI's shareholders with determination. There was another good stock-market operation to back up the Aberdare bid—but not by the Aberdare team itself, mindful of the storm the Philips-Pye market manoeuvring had provoked about City principles. The buying was done by a friendly merchant bank, Morgan Grenfell. With Morgans in support, Aberdare swept to control of Metal Industries, acquiring 53 per cent of the capital by the middle of July 1967. Thorn had been willing to pay more and the Thorn–MI camp were angered by the nature of their defeat. Arguing that the spirit of the City's own rules, if not the letter, had been ignored, they devoted ingenuity and not merely simple wrath to the problem. On the weekend of 15 July 1967 Mr. John Gillum, a director of Kleinwort Benson, MI's merchant bank, pulled out of the hat a solution that set the City ablaze.

The basis of Gillum's scheme was the old British Aluminium technique of issuing new shares in the company to the favoured suitor. The novelty was to do it after control of MI had already been lost. In May 1960, the then shareholders of Metal Industries, at the request of the then board, had approved a large increase in the authorised but unissued share capital. They had it in writing that 'it is not the intention of your directors, without the consent of the ordinary stockholders, to issue any further share capital which would materially affect the control of the company or the nature of its business.'

In July 1967, without asking stockholders' (at that stage Aberdare's) approval, Metal Industries issued almost 5 million new shares to Thorn Electrical in exchange for Thorn's gas appliance manufacturing company, Glover & Main. Of course, the deal was conditional on Thorn gaining full control of MI, so there was no question of Glover and Main actually changing hands. At a stroke of the pen Aberdare's 53 per cent of the MI capital had shrunk to 32 per cent and Thorn put in a higher offer for the rest of the equity. Shareholder democracy was developing into anarchy. Gillum and Kleinworts did not see it that way. 'A careful decision' he said at the time, 'was made for the greatest good of the greatest number. If Thorn had not made this new bid shareholders would have had to take a lower offer from Aberdare. To speak of Aberdare's existing majority was nonsense. The majority was a confused party.' Asked about MI's own undertaking to shareholders back in 1960, he replied that 'to suggest that an intention seven years ago is binding is to do the English language an injustice.'

Gillum still maintains with some eloquence that right was on his side. He was fighting, he claims, against opponents who had not shown strict devotion to the City's good conduct rules; the rules were meant to protect small shareholders and the MI action did that by enabling them to get a better offer from Thorn; and the principle of not issuing unissued shares without express permission was meant to prevent a board of directors from turning itself into a self-perpetuating body, which had obviously not been the intention at MI. 'But ends do not, in our view, justify the means' boomed *The Times* with public opinion on its side. There was one chance to show Kleinworts, Hambros, Metal Industries and Thorn that such behaviour would not be tolerated. The Stock Exchange could refuse permission for the new shares to be issued by MI to Thorn, or by Thorn as payment for its bid, to have a stock-market quotation. There was a snag. Although MI's share issue was very much against the Stock Exchange *General Understanding* of 1966, the Exchange had not called on companies to sign that undertaking until they sought quotation for a new security. Metal Industries had had no need to sign: the Exchange dilemma was whether it could be penalised when it had not done so.

The Stock Exchange Council, always loath to take action which it thought should be the whole City's responsibility, failed to see the extent of the crisis. Although prepared to enter into a public wrangle with *The Times* on the question of what decisions it had communicated, to whom they had been communicated and on which shares, the Council took no action. On Tuesday 18 July *The Times* had made it clear enough what it thought of the affair:

THE CITY CODE

The question of who will fill the shoes the Council fears to put its feet in is not easily answered. The simplest solution would be joint action by interested parties—jobbers, brokers, the Issuing Houses Committee and the institutions—to set up a watchdog organisation on the lines of the U.S. Securities & Exchange Commission. But an effective organisation could not be set up overnight and the free-for-all tactics that have ruled recently need to be stopped soon or the City's already tarnished image will be irretrievably damaged. Until a long term solution can be found in the shape of an S.E.C. or equivalent, general supervision of the stock market might well pass to the Board of Trade.

It was strong stuff, strong enough to be taken up by Prime Minister Harold Wilson at a dinner in the City the same night. 'City headlines in these past days' he said 'have been dominated by a power struggle which has reached spectacular proportions.' But in the Prime Minister's view there were far better ways of taking up parliamentary time than in the promotion of statutory rules—he did not think that it was the government's role to criticise or to take sides. He did, however, make one thing quite clear: 'It is for the City to ensure that these processes are, and are seen to be, carried through in accordance with clearly formulated rules.'

The next evening the Stock Exchange made an announcement:

After consultation with the Governor of the Bank of England, the Stock Exchange has requested the Issuing Houses Association to reconvene as a matter of urgency the Working Party which, in 1959 and 1963, prepared and issued the *Notes on Amalgamations of British Businesses,* and this they have agreed to do. In addition to those represented on the original Working Party, the Confederation of British Industry have now agreed to participate.

It was a last ditch effort to put the house in order and the City took its first steps quickly. Two days later, on 21 July, the executive committee of the Issuing Houses Association drew up broad recommendations for the working party, which held its first meeting on 11 August. The working party, redrew the principles and the procedures of take-over bids, held a second meeting on 25 August; work had begun, it said, on the rules, but 'general agreement was reached on certain other proposals which are being discussed with the Governor of the Bank of England.' The certain other proposals were clear from the newspapers. The working party knew its rules would have no force and they demanded that the

Governor of the Bank of England produce the requisite moral authority by appointing a new watchdog body to do the voluntary policing.

A month later the Bank of England responded with the news that

> on the proposal of the Governor and following discussions with the Chairman of the Issuing Houses Association and the Chairman of the Stock Exchange, and subsequently with the Working Party on Amalgamations and Mergers, agreement has been reached on the establishment of a Panel to supervise the operation of the Code on Amalgamations and Mergers which is currently being revised by the Working Party. At the Governor's request Sir Humphrey Mynors has agreed to serve as first Chairman of the Panel. Membership of the Panel will be drawn from the bodies represented on the Working Party . . . and a permanent secretariat will be provided by the Bank of England. The Panel will come into operation as soon as the work of revising the Code has been completed.

It was a master-stroke of City compromise. There was no indication of the Panel's 'supervisory' powers, there were no rules yet in existence. The Panel's full time—and able—secretary was transferred to this function from the discount office of the Bank of England. And its chairman had for thirty years been a servant of the Bank, ten of them as Deputy Governor; he had begun life as a Cambridge don and crowned a distinguished public career as chairman of the Finance Corporation for Industry and a director of such leading companies as the Legal & General Assurance and English Electric. Tradition was still the key.

While the working party worked and the nascent panel watched, public attention was diverted from the field of regulation by a bid itself—the epic struggle of the then largest merger in the land between GEC and Associated Electrical Industries—and by the economic upheaval of devaluation. Regulation of the stock-market received only passing attention. Metal Industries was forgotten.

3

The 1968 City Code

'It is considered undesirable to fetter the market.' Rule 29, *The City Code on Take-overs and Mergers,* March 1968.

Drafting of the Code

It would be wholly unfair to suggest that the Take-over Code produced by the City working party in March 1968 was in any sense amateur. It was strictly an insiders' job and the insiders were professionals—not the institutional representatives on the working party but four merchant bankers advising the working party with a background of training in the new issue and merger business of their houses.

Heading the quartet was Mr. Michael Bucks of Rothschilds and Mr. Ken Barrington of Morgan Grenfell, respectively chairman and deputy chairman of the Issuing Houses Association executive committee, the merchant bankers' society. Rothschilds had, back in 1963, been the controversial advisers of Richard Thomas & Baldwins and provoked the revision of the old general *Notes on Amalgamations.* Morgans had stood behind Aberdare in the battle for Metal Industries which had provoked the call for this, a sterner, code. Bucks, a Rothschild man all his life, had risen to partnership in that closely guarded family bank. Barrington was a professional accountant who had moved into banking. With these two were Mr. Robert Clark, head of the mergers and issues business of Hill, Samuel; and, the odd man out in this big league company, Mr. Peter Cannon, boss of a new finance house which had only recently acquired bank status, Minster Trust.

Clark had moved into merchant banking after eight years as a partner in one of the City's most prestigious solicitors, Slaughter and May. At Slaughters he had already been blooded in the take-over business. At Hill, Samuel while the Code was in preparation he had guided Arnold Weinstock and GEC to a hard fought and hard won victory over Associated Electrical Industries. Cannon on the other hand had been much criticised in the City for the way in which his Minster Trust had priced new issues of shares to establish large rises in their share prices in early dealings on the stock-market. His inclusion in the team, it was suggested, was simply to balance appearances with a non-establishment figure from a minor bank. It was a misjudgement of character. When the four found themselves at loggerheads with the full working party on the sweeping changes they proposed, it was alleged to be Cannon who did the arguing and the persuading that the Code should not be emasculated.

Rules and Principles

The rules were certainly clear, forceful and reasonable, and the general principles with which the Code opened spelt out the new mood. 'Inevitably' said the first paragraph 'these principles and the ensuing rules will impinge on the freedom of action of boards and persons involved in such (take-over) transactions.' They did so. The principles were stern enough:

At no time . . . shall any action be taken by the board of the offeree company, without the approval in general meeting of the shareholders of the offeree company, which could effectively result in any bona fide offer being frustrated or in the shareholders of the offeree company being denied an opportunity to decide on its merits.

Notwithstanding the legal rights of a majority anything done to oppress a minority (in the general and not only the legal sense of the words) is wholly unacceptable.

Any document or advertisement addressed to shareholders containing information, opinions and recommendations from the boards of an offeror or an offeree company or their respective advisers shall be treated with the same standards of care as if it were a prospectus within the meaning of the Companies Act 1948.

The rules which followed dealt with specific areas of contention, defining what could or could not be done by companies, their advisers and their 'friends' when dealing in the stock-market; providing for disclosure of these dealings and other vital facts like cross-shareholdings and directors' service contracts; prohibiting an unpenalised free-for-all in the market, inequality of treatment for any group of shareholders or bids for less than half a company's capital; and laying down a much stricter control on the euphoric way in which companies produced forecasts of their profits in the course of a bid.

All the old problems were taken care of. By Rule 20 no company was allowed to declare its bid unconditional unless it had acquired shares carrying over 50 per cent of the voting rights of the ordinary capital. Courtaulds for example could not have shut its bid for Wilkinson & Riddell with only 29 per cent acceptance and then created havoc in the stock-market with its buying spree.

By Rule 26 bids for less than the complete capital of a company were frowned on, but, it they were made, arrangements had to be drawn up to enable every shareholder to accept for the same proportion of his holding. Open market tenders on a first-come-first-served basis, as in the struggle for Cook & Watts, were out. What was more, the old bugbear of special terms or selling arrangements for particular shareholders—that is, the large and powerful institutions—were outlawed. 'Since purchases' said Rule 32 'with special conditions attached are not capable in every circumstance of being extended to all shareholders, such purchases whether during, or in anticipation of, a bid must not be made.'

The procedure of carving up a company or its capital, begun with British Aluminium and smartened up by Metal Industries, was banned in the clearest terms. In the jargon of Rule 34

> During the course of an offer, or even before the date of the offer if the board of the offeree company has reason to believe that a bona fide offer is imminent, the board must not, without the approval of shareholders in general meeting, issue any authorised but unissued shares or sell, dispose of or acquire or agree to sell, dispose of or acquire assets of material amount or enter into material contracts otherwise than in the ordinary course of business.

Although no move was made to ban stock-market transactions in the course of a bid ('It is considered undesirable to fetter the market'), the heaviest hand of the new code fell on such dealings. All parties to an offer had to inform the Stock Exchange and the Press of how many shares they had bought and sold and what average price by midday on the working day following such a transaction. What is more, if the price paid in the market was above the official bid price, as in the Wilkinson & Riddell case, the price paid to all shareholders had to be no lower than the *weighted average* price of market transactions. The old *Notes on Amalgamations* had left that issue delightfully vague by suggesting 'a fair price' taking into account market dealings.

THE 1968 CITY CODE

The real loophole, moreover, was plugged by including under this set of rules the associates of parties to a bid. The Code defined associates as a term intended to cover 'all parties (whether or not acting in concert with the offeror or offeree company) who deal in the shares of the offeror or offeree company in a bid situation and who have (in addition to their normal interest as a shareholder) any interest or potential interest, whether commercial, financial or personal, in the outcome of an offer.' Apart from naming the generally obvious candidates, such as bankers, financial advisers, directors, and pension funds, the Code added to the definition 'any company or individual acquiring during the course of a bid an interest which together with any holding it had at the outset of the bid represents 10 per cent or more of the equity capital of the offeror or offeree company.' And for all such associates there was the warning that, under Rule 33, if their dealings 'could affect the outcome of a bid in circumstances in which the associate has an existing or potential financial or commercial interest in the success or otherwise of the offer, then such associate must be prepared to satisfy the Panel that his action was not prejudicial to the interests of shareholders generally of the offeror or the offeree company as the case may be.' In effect, the days of market operations like the Pye share build-up, or the subsequent aid given to International Distillers & Vintners by Watney Mann in fighting off a bid from Showerings, were numbered. While IDV was busy trying to repulse a bid from Showerings in 1967, a mysterious buyer in the stockmarket, later to emerge as Watney Mann, amassed a significant proportion of the company's shares and sided with the board in rejecting Showerings' terms.

The Code went further than these provisions on other important matters. Companies in bids had to declare their shareholdings in each other at the outset and to enumerate the holdings and service contracts of their directors. When effective control was held by a board, or shareholders who had a say on the board, they were strongly recommended not to sell such a controlling interest without making sure the same terms were made available by a general offer to all other shareholders. Finally, profit forecasts were made subject to some sort of scrutiny.

A company's projections had to be corroborated, together with the assumptions on which they were based, by its merchant bank or financial adviser, while the auditors or consultant accountants had to examine and report on the calculations and bases of the forecasts. These reports had to be made in writing to the company's board of directors. Circulars to shareholders only had to state the assumptions on which the forecasts were based and reveal the latest unaudited profits for any trading period which had already begun and for which a forecast was being made. But the Code at least implied that optimism had henceforth to be tempered with logic. Cumulatively the provisions of the Code drawn up by four merchant bankers were probably more stringent than most observers of the City had expected or than statutory rules could have been. By the newspapers that had howled for it, the Code was greeted with enthusiasm. 'Sweeping takeover changes in tough new rules for the City' said the headline in *The Times* and it called its leading article 'A momentous stride forward for the City'.

But there was one gap in what otherwise looked like regulation as tough as the American securities markets had been subjected to more than thirty years earlier. 'All that is now needed' said *The Times* 'is that the Code should be implemented. It is up to the Panel and those bodies represented on it to see that the Code is kept. The Bank of England has put the full weight of its authority —halfway between Government and City—behind the Code.'

The same question posed itself to the *Financial Times*: 'A short sharp crunch with a transgressor in the near future with the Bank in full cry would be the best possible way of showing the Panel means business. After all, by itself the Panel is practically toothless. With the single exception of saying that contravention of Clause 24 on the declaration of acceptances could be dealt with by a (Stock Exchange) suspension of (share) dealings the Code remains silent about sanctions.' But Michael Bucks, author-in-chief of the rules, felt simply that 'the City should discipline itself. This is our last chance before legislation.'

4

The Panel on Trial

'While there has been constructive as well as destructive criticism, notice has mainly been taken of those few cases—five bids out of some 500—where the Panel has issued formal statements for publication. Naturally these have far more immediate news value, if not intrinsic importance for the proper conduct of take-over bids, than rulings which have been given to and accepted by the parties, rulings often of a technical character. There is therefore no ground for complaint in this: but it can easily lead to a false inference, that the only test of the Panel is whether the Inspector gets his Man.' *Report on the year ended* 31 *March* 1969 *of The Panel on Take-overs and Mergers.*

'The cult of the gifted amateur is the new Take-over Panel's main defect. It has no teeth, no legal sanctions—in fact, to me it's all a kind of confidence trick.' Sir Frank Kearton, chairman of Courtaulds, in a television interview, 27 June 1968.

Courtaulds, Dufay and International Paints

The City's new police force went to work in April 1968, a year unprecedented for the number and size of take-over bids in Britain. After devaluation of the pound at the end of 1967 the political stress on exports and internationally competitive industrial units made giganticism positively fashionable. At the same time the stock-market boom, boosting the value of almost every company's shares, permitted the process of acquisition to be relatively painless: take-overs did not have to be paid for in cash but in paper, the highly valued shares of acquisitive companies. It was almost a self-generating procedure. The greater the number of bids, the faster the market rose in the expectation of more bids; the more a company displayed its dynamic philosophy by entering the take-over lists to expand, the higher its share price went. Inevitably before the year was out the Panel would have to face more than one 'short sharp crunch' with or without the Bank of England in full cry. Ironically its first test was the third episode in what took on the appearance of a continuing saga, one which had helped bring the Panel into being in the first place.

Crossing swords again were John Gommes of P. P. Rodocanachi and Rodo Investment Trust (backed by the I.C.I. pension fund and the Bankers Trust of New York), and Sir Frank Kearton, chairman of Courtaulds and then of the Industrial Reorganisation Corporation. The object of their affections on this occasion was not a textile company, but International Paints.

Courtaulds already had one of the country's largest paint companies, Pinchin Johnson Associates. Gommes had a large stake in and had masterminded the expansion of a relatively small paint firm, Dufay. Dufay's shares, on the strength of some heady profit forecasts from the Gommes camp, was one of the 1968 stock-market high flyers and its bid for International Paints was an attempt to use that market rating to break into the big league. Kearton and the rest of the big league already had ideas on how the vast number of manufacturing and marketing companies in the industry could be usefully reduced and concentrated. However, when Gommes went after International Paints, Kearton, despite an interest in buying the company, was obviously not anxious to have another take-over battle. When Dufay increased its bid price in the knowledge that Kearton was sniffing the wind, Kearton himself, it emerged in due course, could scarcely credit that anybody would take a Dufay bid seriously.

There were certainly problems at Dufay. The company despatched its offer document for International Paints on 6 May 1968, in which it forecast that the Dufay profits for the twelve month accounting period to the end of September would rise from £327,000 to something in the region of £500,000, even though the paints division would do more than maintain its previous earnings. International and its advisers, Lazards, countered with the obvious tactic of pointing out to shareholders that Dufay had not been able to produce any actual progress figures, only forecasts, 'in spite of the fact that seven months of Dufay's trading year are past.' On 28 May 1968, two days before increasing his bid and extending it to 7 June 1968, Gommes and co-directors at Dufay 'made no apology' for not producing half-year profit figures for the months that had passed on the grounds that accounting progress had been disrupted by the concentration of the group's various paint producing operations in a single new factory at Shildon and the establishment of a single sales force, described as 'an immense task.' A week later, however, the papers reported that Mr. G. L. Mortimer, chief accountant of Dufay's paints division had resigned and gone to earth. Mr. Mortimer in fact disappeared under the Press's nose that same day, 4 June 1968, into the offices of the Take-over Panel in the Bank of England.

There he pointed out that he had long ago prepared a provisional profits statement for Dufay's paints division for the first quarter of its trading year, the seasonally bad three months to the end of December 1967. The figures circulated to the board of the paint subsidiary at the end of March showed a loss of £9,000. Mortimer added that he had been asked to prepare forecasts for the current year and the next year at twenty-four hours' notice in connection with the bid. The holding company's auditors had, he said, found the paints division forecast for 1967–68 'too optimistic'. In fact the auditors halved the projection, making the revised paint division forecast 21 per cent lower than its actual results for the previous year. This revised projection was the basis of Dufay's bid statement that the paint division's profits for 1967–68 'would not be materially different from those for the previous year.' Mortimer went further. On 28 May 1968, the day Gommes and the rest of the board had made no apology for not presenting up-to-date results for Dufay, the paint subsidiary directors had been circulated with a provisional result for the six months to the end of March, showing a loss of about £30,000 compared with a profit of about £49,000 for the same six months of the year before. These figures, Mortimer stressed, stated the gloomiest view since the group might charge reorganisation expenditure included in the losses to future years' profits—an accountancy practice which they had followed and shown clearly before.

But the burden of Mortimer's talk with the Panel was obvious. Sir Humphrey Mynors and his colleagues were in a quandary; the Code said that 'the Panel cannot be expected to pronounce on the merits or demerits of any individual offer' and Sir Humphrey and the rest of the Panel viewed their job as interpreters of the Code not as a sort of accountancy principles board.

That day they got in touch with Rodo and Gommes to observe that Dufay's circulars of 28 May and 30 May did not reiterate the formal acceptance of responsibility by the board and suggested that the statement of 6 May on the absence of actual profit figures for the year in progress be brought up to date. Next day Gommes complied. Although interim figures were not available because of the production upheaval, the board of Dufay confirmed on 5 June that profits for the year to the end of September 1968 would be of the order of £500,000, and not less than £800,000 for the following year—and again accepted responsibility for all the statements of fact and opinion in all their circulars to shareholders. On 6 June Mortimer went back to the Panel with his supporting documents to be interviewed by Sir Humphrey Mynors himself. The day after, Gommes once again extended his bid for another twelve days—to 19 June—and Sir Humphrey asked him 'for an early discussion'.

The meeting took place on 11 June, Gommes saying at the start that he accepted 'personal responsibility' for everything which had been done on behalf of Dufay. He made it clear that the figures which Mortimer had been discussing were regarded as management accounts only and not of the quality for use in official statements. He had been told, he said, of Mortimer's six months figures for the paint division but when these had been examined by the auditors of the Dufay holding company 'they were found to contain errors, as well as to require adjustments, which took time particularly after the resignation of the chief accountant. It was already possible to see that when these corrections and adjustments had been made the outcome would look very different.' The upshot was that, despite difficulties in both the paint and bitumastic divisions of Dufay, Gommes hoped to be able to publish half-yearly figures for the company before his offer for International Paints expired.

The Panel welcomed the news. They did more than that, however, turning the results of their inquiries over to the Press on 13 June, though adding the disclaimer that 'the Panel express no opinion on the likely outcome of the current year in relation to the published forecast of the total profits nor is it their function to examine the detailed figures of particular companies.' It was the first public pronouncement by the City's new watchdog and it was a sensation. Evaluating the effect is beyond precision, but it was generally accepted that Gommes was sunk.

Less than a week later Kearton and Courtaulds moved in for the kill. On 18 June, a mere day before Dufay's offer was due to close (in which context it is worth noting that institutions tend not to accept or reject bids until literally the last possible moment), Courtaulds and its merchant bankers Hill, Samuel declared their intention to make a bid for International Paints. What they omitted to mention, just when a final decision had to be taken on the Dufay offer, was how much they were willing to pay. Advising Courtaulds at Hill, Samuel was Robert Clark, one of the four men who had written the Code: and Rule 14 of the Code insisted that 'shareholders must be put in possession of all the facts necessary for an informed judgement as to the merits or demerits of an offer. Such facts must be accurately and fairly presented and be available to the shareholders early enough to enable them to make a decision in good time'.

The Panel Tries Censure

Sir Humphrey Mynors responded with a public rap over the knuckles for Courtaulds and Hill, Samuel. Gommes had meanwhile lost the fight when his bid closed without sufficient acceptances, but Kearton lost his composure nonetheless. He had stormed round to the Stock Exchange almost exactly a year earlier to ask for an enquiry into the Wilkinson & Riddell affair. This time he stormed round to Sir Leslie O'Brien, Governor of the Bank of England, complaining that the Panel had published its findings on the Courtaulds breach of the Code without consulting the company and demanding an enquiry into the way the Panel operated.

Kearton then entertained a packed Press conference at Courtaulds' Hanover Square headquarters with a bitter attack on several targets. The Stock Exchange, and its inactivity on Wilkinson & Riddell, was one. The investing institutions, with so much money to invest that they had an exaggerated idea of what companies were worth, were another. The Dufay offer for International Paints, he said, Courtaulds could not regard as serious and the Dufay share price was artificially high. Also under fire came the accountancy profession, since neither the investing institutions nor by implication a bidder had any real information on the true status of the companies they bought. In sum, he wanted a British Securities & Exchange Commission to police share dealings and company affairs.

American Fight for Gallaher

As the affairs of International Paints occupied the take-over strategists, one of the largest offerings of ordinary shares was made to the investing public. It was not a new issue. The company concerned, the country's second largest cigarette producer, produced brands such as Benson & Hedges, Senior Service, Piccadilly and Guards. This was Gallaher, already quoted on the stock-market and widely held by the public.

The biggest shareholder in Gallaher, however, was the giant Imperial Tobacco (Players and Wills) whose sizable holding of 36 per cent or 26 million shares in its main competitor had long since drawn the unwelcome attention of the Monopolies Commission. Beside that the 13 per cent of Gallaher held by American Tobacco looked small stuff. For some time Imperial, diversifying fast in the food industry, had maintained that it regarded its shares in Gallaher as 'disposable'. In May 1968 to the surprise of outsiders it moved to dispose of them by a public offer for sale at 20s. a share. American Tobacco expressed no interest and the British public little more—the underwriters of the issue, headed by bankers Morgan Grenfell, were left with more than a third of the stock. Gallaher had been losing its market share to Imperial and, with tobacco duties rising, lung cancer widely publicised and television advertising of cigarettes banned, tobacco shares were not highly favoured by investors.

A few weeks later, on 26 June 1968, Philip Morris of the United States, having sized up its compatriot's, American Tobacco's, disinterest, amazed the British market with an offer of 25s. a share for half of Gallaher's ordinary capital. Despite the flop of the Imperial issued at 20s., Mr. Mark Norman, chairman of Gallaher and a director of merchant bankers Lazards, dismissed the Philip Morris terms as 'quite unacceptable.' Philip Morris and its bankers S. G. Warburg were in no hurry. They decided to see what sort of profit forecast Gallaher could produce before thinking again.

It was an unproductive wait. On 16 July American Tobacco declared its resolve to protect its investment in Gallaher from Philip Morris and, advised by Morgan Grenfell, counter-bid 35s. a share for half of the British company's capital. The new team lost no time. The same morning London's largest stockbrokers, Cazenove, acting under Morgan's instructions, mopped up more than 12 million Gallaher shares in an hour or two at a fraction under American's bid price, giving American virtual control of the company.

The nature of that transaction let all hell loose. Morgan and Cazenove did not stage a conventional stock-market operation; as underwriters to the Imperial offer of Gallaher they knew exactly which City institutions had bundles of (unwanted) shares taken at 20s. a few weeks earlier. The lucky institutions on the network were quickly relieved of their entire holdings of Gallaher at 35s. a share—everybody else was being offered that price for only half their shares, with the other half apparently worth no more than 25s. in the open market at the time.

The Panel hardly needed reminding of Principle 7 of the Code:

... In particular, after a bid is reasonably in contemplation, there shall not be made to a shareholder of an offeree company an offer which is more favourable than a general offer to be made thereafter to the other shareholders of the same class.

The principle of equality in the shareholder democracy, after all, was the shrine to which the Code and the Panel did obeisance. The blue-blooded houses of Morgan Grenfell, chairman Lord Harcourt, and of Cazenove, senior partner Sir Antony Hornby, were asked to explain their buying on behalf of American Tobacco.

They argued that the Code's rules on share purchases in the market had not been tested before in a partial bid and that in this sort of situation Principle 7, cited by the Panel, seemed to be in direct conflict with Rule 29 ('It is considered undesirable to fetter the market. Accordingly, all parties to a take-over or merger transaction and their associates are free to deal at arm's length, subject to daily disclosure . . .').

Ironically, the Panel's chairman to decide this recurring and key question of market dealings was none other than the boss of the market itself, Stock Exchange chairman Sir Martin Wilkinson. The normal chairman, Sir Humphrey Mynors, had stood down throughout the Gallaher affair on the grounds that, as a director of Imperial Tobacco, he faced a potential conflict of interest. Under Wilkinson's leadership the Panel made its opinion clear and terse—in what amounted to its first public censure it concluded that 'certain dealings in Gallaher shares' constituted a breach of the Code.

City Argument with the Panel

The Panel may have considered that such a form of censure, canvassed as a powerful weapon when the Code was drawn up, would end the matter. But Morgans and Cazenove were outraged by the rebuke and countered immediately with the opinion that they could not 'agree with the conclusions of the Panel since both are firmly of the view that, so far as they are concerned, they have complied with the Code in every respect.' It was a head-on clash between the City's voice of authority and the City's most authoritative leaders, and neither could afford to back down.

After a week's talking, the Panel spoke again in what at first sounded like the voice of compromise. For their part Lord Harcourt of Morgan Grenfell and Sir Antony Hornby of Cazenove had changed their fighting stance and wished 'to refute any implication' that their initial reaction suggested they 'contemplated flouting the authority of the Panel'. Indeed, they added, they would always comply with a definite Panel ruling. For its part, the Panel accepted that both eminent houses had acted in good faith 'in their belief that such dealings were within the letter and spirit of the Code'. Moreover, it agreed to examine their argument on Rule 29 and Principle 7 under a process of reviewing the Code's provisions. There was, however, a sting in the tail. The Panel repeated its opinion that the Code had been breached and had 'so informed the Stock Exchange and the Issuing Houses Association'. In plain English, the Panel could do nothing about it and referred the case to the only voluntary disciplinary bodies which could. If the Code was to work, action had to be taken.

Despite its chairman's leadership of the Panel in this test case, the Stock Exchange Council wavered. At the end of nearly three weeks it decided that Cazenove's buying of Gallaher shares had breached the Code but in the same breath it cleared the firm of any blame. There was no evidence to suggest, the Council said, that Cazenove 'knew or should have known at the time in the confused and competitive bid situation that they were in any danger of breaching the City Code by their actions.' At the Issuing Houses Association the merchant bankers were having no easier time in deciding what to say about their colleague Morgan Grenfell. Two meetings had been held without any result by 14 August, the day the Stock Exchange announced its Cazenove verdict.

THE PANEL ON TRIAL

It was more than public opinion could stand and the City knew it. Within twenty-four hours the Governor of the Bank of England, Sir Leslie O'Brien, intervened with an open letter to Michael Bucks at the Issuing Houses Association, Sir Martin Wilkinson at the Stock Exchange and Sir Humphrey Mynors at the Panel. A 'disappointed' Sir Leslie threatened the City with the ultimate weapon, legislation. 'If the present arrangements prove inadequate' he said 'no doubt some form of statutory control will be considered.'

Acknowledging that the Code may need continuous revision and clarification, he reminded his audience that it was not a legal document but one of guidance—dependent for its effectiveness on those who use it subscribing to and understanding the objectives of the machinery. If that sounded like the City's theme-song on voluntary regulation, the rest of Sir Leslie's letter left no doubt on where he was pointing a finger and what he planned to do about it:

> The purpose of the Panel is to give authoritative rulings on the interpretation of the Code and, so far as possible, to secure that these rulings are respected. . . . In a few instances, after due deliberation, the Panel has felt obliged to state publicly that a breach of the Code has in its opinion occurred. In my view these rulings were in each case entirely justified and I do not see that the Panel had any option but to make them public and to do so with the minimum of delay. The result, however, has been less than satisfactory. Much resentment has been aroused. The Panel's rulings have been questioned and even their general authority has not always been acknowledged. It is in no one's interest that this state of affairs should continue.

The point at issue was made painfully obvious.

> I know that the Panel are considering their methods and procedures. . . . Both Sir Humphrey Mynors and I will welcome any suggestions which you may have. I hope these will not exclude proposals for effective sanctions against wilful infringements of the Code.

Nine days later the Issuing Houses Association published its conclusions on Morgan Grenfell's role in the affair. There was no question of sanction but no mincing of words. The executive committee of the IHA regarded 'with great concern the attitude towards the Panel which appears to have been adopted by Morgan Grenfell following upon the ruling in question'. Lord Harcourt replied to convey Morgan's 'sincerest regret that anything said or done in

33

recent weeks should have resulted in the Committee coming to the view you have expressed.' The horse, however, had already bolted. While Gallaher itself passed quietly into the history of take-overs and the control of American Tobacco, the word 'sanctions' had entered the official language of the City.

5

Demise of the Old Panel

'As you know I have been severely criticised in many media; I have been much criticised but one thing I have not been criticised for is lacking in ideas or energy.' Mr. Robert Maxwell, M.C., M.P., chairman and managing director of Pergamon Press.

Toning Down a Censure

The post-mortem on the bids for Gallaher exposed not the weakness of the Take-over Panel but the weaknesses of the system in which it was being asked to operate. It has been argued within the City that the Governor of the Bank of England himself, while demanding stricter obedience and fiercer rules, had contributed to that state of affairs. While his public intervention in the proceedings effectively called on the Issuing Houses Association to censure the house of Morgan Grenfell, the City working party from whom he had demanded new rules and ideas on sanctions may have felt that Sir Leslie O'Brien simultaneously had weakened the case by not objecting to an arrangement which might appear to have toned down the censure.

The difficulty lay within the IHA itself. Its annual meeting and rotation of executive office was due to be held before the end of November 1968. At that stage Michael Bucks of Rothschilds should have stepped down from the chairmanship of the IHA and his deputy chairman, Mr. Ken Barrington of Morgan Grenfell, should have taken over. The succession was not, some argued, consistent with an official IHA censure of Morgans. If censure there had to be, then it would be necessary for Barrington to forfeit the IHA chairmanship if the censure was not to be seen as a form of public joke. One side of the logic was clearly accepted, but this elementary form of sanction was not enforced. To avoid what may have looked severe action, the IHA changed its meeting from 30 November to 31 March and, at the same time, agreed that all its executive offices should be extended by a 'year' to the March 1970 period. By that time it was hoped Gallaher and the censure of Morgan Grenfell in the summer of 1968 would have been forgotten and Barrington would be able to assume the Association's chairmanship without being singled out as a victim of the City's new disciplinary authorities.

How far this arrangement might have weakened attitudes within the Panel and the rest of the City, it is impossible to say. Certainly the Panel, which had so far acted with firmness, failed its next test miserably. In the corporate and merchant banking worlds, attacker and attacked, aggressor and victim, change their roles with almost baffling speed. On this occasion the merchant bank of Hill, Samuel, acting with the smaller house of Robert Fleming, felt that they and their client, Mr. Robert Maxwell, the Labour M.P. and millionaire chief of publishing house Pergamon Press, were the unfortunate victims of the Panel's inaction. It was to prove a supreme irony.

Expansion of Pergamon Press

Maxwell had founded his Pergamon business, his second incursion into the publishing industry since the war, on a highly successful launch of innumerable scientific journals. A remarkably favourable selling agreement with Macmillan of New York, which lasted for three years between 1962 and 1965, allowed a rapid expansion in the publishing of textbooks.

Early in 1966 Pergamon, which two years earlier had achieved a stock-market quotation that valued the company at £3.5m, spread its wings. Maxwell paid £1m for the subscription book publishing interests of George Newnes, whose principal product was Chambers Encyclopaedia. In the middle of 1967 Pergamon bought out another subscription book company, Caxton Publishing, which had run foul of the Consumer Council for its selling methods, and shortly afterwards set the seal on its interests in the field by merging them with those of the British Printing Corporation in a jointly owned subsidiary, the International Learning Systems Corporation. I.L.S.C. quickly pushed its sales overseas and in due course provoked a certain amount of hostility—in Australia, for instance, the operation was subject to a savage attack from the newspaper publishing empire of local Press magnate Mr. Rupert Murdoch. Meanwhile, however, Maxwell was anxious to expand Pergamon's other interests by acquisition. He lost an animated battle over publishers Butterworths to the International Publishing Corporation, the Daily Mirror group which had sold him the Newnes business: and in the autumn of 1968 he decided to go after a major national newspaper, the *News of the World*.

News of the World was a public company with two classes of ordinary shares, those that carried votes and those that did not. The voting shares were still controlled by the founding families of the enterprise, but the families, as Maxwell well knew, were not united. Sir William Carr, chairman of News of the World, could muster 30 per cent of the votes. But Professor Derek Jackson, who had retired to Switzerland and was represented in London by Rothschilds, had an almost parallel 26 per cent.

By the time Maxwell had instructed his bankers Hill, Samuel and Flemings and launched a £26¾m bid for News of the World on 16 October 1968, he had won Jackson round and 26 per cent of the votes were committed to Pergamon. Hostility to Maxwell, however, was not uncommon in the publishing and printing industry; he had never been well received since the collapse of the book wholesaling company of Simpkin Marshall in the early 1950s. At News of the World Sir William Carr called in his bankers Hambros and rejected Maxwell's bid. Carr needed allies since the company's profit record and share price history would not necessarily inspire loyalty in the face of a good bid.

News of the World and Pergamon

In Australia an energetic and expansionist Rupert Murdoch, chief shareholder and drive force behind News Ltd. hurriedly contacted Morgan Grenfell in London to see if he could get in on the News of the World act. Morgans worked on it.

Maxwell upped his bid within a few days to £34m but the forces ranged against him were at work in the stock-market. The major of these was Hambros Bank, which had informed the Takeover Panel that it was out buying on its own account. In a week between 16 October and 22 October Hambros was able to acquire 11.8 per cent of the News of the World voting shares with the Panel's knowledge. The danger of the situation should have been apparent. Since Sir William Carr and his associates had 30 per cent, and the Maxwell-Jackson camp 26 per cent, only 44 per cent of the NoW voting equity was there to chase. Hambros got more than a quarter of it and put the Carr side up to almost 42 per cent of the votes. With purchases on that scale the danger was that the entrenched board and its associates, by buying in the stock-market, would be able to repulse any Maxwell offer obstinately and the rest of the News of the World's shareholders would see a valuable offer frustrated.

The shock for the Panel came on 24 October. Morgan Grenfell had entered the market too on behalf of Rupert Murdoch and bought a further 3½ per cent. With additional pledges of a further 7 per cent of the voting shares, Carr and Murdoch revealed that they had formed a seemingly improbable alliance, commanded more than half the News of the World votes, and would propose a scheme to shareholders (of which they constituted a voting majority) that would give Murdoch's Australian company 40 per cent of an expanded News of the World voting capital in return for certain important but unspecified assets.

Too late the alliance was seen to have disposed of Maxwell's bid before even considering it, making nonsense of the Code's intentions if not its actual dictat under Principle 3: that nothing should be done without the approval of shareholders that would frustrate an offer or deny shareholders an opportunity to decide on its merits. At 10.30 on the morning of the 24th the Panel, long since informed of Morgan's entry into the market on behalf of Murdoch, had in fact requested that Morgan stop its buying. But Lord Catto, the director of the bank handling the affair, made it clear that he 'was reluctant to do so because many shareholders were still willing to take advantage of the good prices offered.' The burden of Murdoch's and Catto's case was that the proposed deal with News Ltd. would make the News of the World's shares worth at least the 50s. being offered by Maxwell. By 2.30 p.m., when it had asked all parties to the affair to withdraw from the market and requested a suspension of dealings by the Stock Exchange Council, the Panel had got itself in an impossible position. If, having stopped market dealings too late in the day, there was one issue to decide—whether the spirit of the Code had been observed by a NoW-News alliance offering a deal as valuable as Maxwell's bid—then the Panel was pushing itself into the one role it specifically wanted to avoid, that of judging specific bid terms and the value of complex transactions. If in the News of the World case it failed to assume that role, then the outside shareholders of News of the World could only conclude *prima facie* that they had lost the chance of a good bid and that the Panel had failed to protect their interest.

That sounded the Panel's death knell. Sir Leslie O'Brien had said at a dinner at the Mansion House the week before that he thought it unreasonable to expect the Governor of the Bank 'to intervene personally and publicly in every instance where trouble arises.' Before the Panel reached its conclusions on the News of the World, Sir Leslie had presented the major City institutions with a new set of proposals for a substantially new Panel—that it should be a body with a full-time head from a merchant bank, that there should be a larger, full-time staff with offices apart from the Bank of England, that the Code should again be redrafted, and finally that, as he had hinted at the time of the Gallaher case, there should be a new and more positive form of sanction for transgression of the Code. The President of the Board of Trade joined in: Mr. Anthony Crosland, after a meeting with Sir Leslie, agreed that they had discussed the possible reinforcement of new controls by the Board and that he and the Governor had agreed to remain in touch on the general subject. The omens for voluntary regulation were bad.

The next day the Panel detailed its intervention into the News of the World affair—it had secured the agreement of Hambros, Morgan Grenfell and Hill, Samuel not to vote the shares they had bought in the stock-market since Robert Maxwell's first bid when an extraordinary general meeting of News of the World was called on to decide whether or not to approve the projected deal between NoW and Murdoch's News Ltd.

For the Maxwell-Hill, Samuel team that was a hollow victory. Not only was it held that the Code had not been breached, but the mere neutralisation of Hambros and Morgans did not restore the status quo. Although they could not vote, the fact that their share dealings were not unwound meant that virtually all the uncommitted holdings would have to support Maxwell to give him any chance of success. Moreover, the Panel's decision to suspend the votes for NoW's extraordinary meeting might allow Maxwell a slim chance of blocking the deal with Murdoch: it did not follow that he could achieve his original and only real aim, to win control of News of the World with his take-over bid.

Proposals for a New Panel

For one brief moment it looked as though the problem of sanctions for breaches of the Code was to be tackled with determination. Indeed, five days after the Panel's ruling Mr. Anthony Crosland, President of the Board of Trade, returned to the subject in a reply to a House of Commons question. Announcing that neither the Pergamon Press bid for News of the World nor the News Ltd. alternative proposals would be referred to the Monopolies Commission, Crosland added that recent take-over events had given rise to 'acute anxiety and disquiet'; if a reshaped voluntary system on the lines he had discussed with Sir Leslie O'Brien still proved inadequate, he 'would not hesitate to take statutory powers.'

At every stage of take-over control, however, the appropriate authorities had backed away from the determined action that should have followed logically from their declarations of intent. It had happened time and again at the Stock Exchange. It was arguable that it had happened on the single important instance with the Issuing Houses Association, to which the Governor of the Bank of England had not objected. It was now the government's turn. Within days of Crosland's House of Commons answer, Prime Minister Harold Wilson toned down Crosland's menacing words when he addressed the entire City at the Lord Mayor's Guildhall banquet. 'The government has no desire' he said 'to introduce legislation to force on the City the much tougher and more wide-ranging interference which free-enterprise America has devised in the form of the Securities and Exchange Commission or indeed in any other form, for this job is far better done by the City.' Wilson did observe that the job was not being done effectively; that unless shareholders' rights were upheld the free flow of investment capital could be restricted; and that recent events had cast a shadow over the working of some of the country's institutions. But the crux of the matter was that although highly publicised and unfairly fought take-overs were a 'matter of government concern', it was his hope that they would not have to become 'a matter for government action.'

DEMISE OF THE OLD PANEL

On 2 January a packed meeting of shareholders of News of the World clamoured support for their board of directors and voted overwhelmingly in support of Sir William Carr's proposals for the link with Murdoch and News Ltd. Robert Maxwell was booed and hissed as he tried to address the meeting. In due course Hambros Bank sold their shares without loss to News Ltd. and Rupert Murdoch now sits in voting control of News of the World. Sir William Carr has retired. Months later Mr. Maxwell turned his attention to another national newspaper when he offered to relieve the International Publishing Corporation of the loss-making *Sun*. The *Sun* negotiations collapsed and the paper passed into the control of the News of the World organisation and its new managing director Mr. Rupert Murdoch.

6
The 1969 City Code

'Save in so far as appears from this Code, it is considered undesirable to fetter the market.' *The City Code on Take-overs and Mergers*, Revised edition 28 April 1969.

New Panel Staff

Given the unseemly demise of the first City Code and the drastic reshaping of the first City Panel within a year of their establishment, there were and remain only three serious questions about the value and limitations of their successors. First, the nature and effectiveness of the new Panel staff. Second, the changes in the rules they were asked to operate. Third, the nature of the sanctions they could use to back up their decisions.

Before the end of February 1969 Sir Leslie O'Brien was able to reveal his new Panel team. The fact that the chairmanship of that body was styled non-executive did not detract from the nature of the appointments. The chairman who accepted that office was Lord Shawcross, politely described as a forceful personality—in his day one of the best known lawyers in practice, a star of the post-war Labour government, and subsequently a protagonist of the movement for Wider Share Ownership and a director of such giant industrial companies as Shell and Electric & Musical Industries. The merchant bankers were hardly likely to forget his powers of interrogation or his legendary post-war political phrase, 'we are the masters now.'

Beside Shawcross there were also ranged the equally important changes in the Panel structure, the creation of a full-time executive director general and his deputy. Taking over the director general's seat was a professional merchant banker, Mr. Ian Fraser, a 45-year-old director of S. G. Warburg. Fraser was not the traditional mould of City man. He had worked for Reuters news agency throughout Europe and been chief of their Geneva bureau before deciding that journalism was too exhausting. Turning to the City, he said 'everyone told me I should go to Siegmund Warburg.' He went and became a director of the bank in 1961, specialising in international business before turning to the hurly burly of new issues and take-overs.

As vital to the initial operations of the Panel was Fraser's deputy, Mr. Wilfred Wareham. Wareham, aged 60, was seconded to the job from the Stock Exchange where he was and is probably the Exchange's most important paid official, secretary of the Quotations Department, after a lifetime career with the Exchange. The job may be unknown outside the City, but Wareham has been described as the force behind the scenes in improving the Exchange's demands for disclosure of information from companies—and in prodding the company directors who were unwilling to comply.

The significance of this double harness was that effective policing of the merger business repeatedly centred on the stock-market itself and the brokers who acted there for the merchant banks. 'Close liaison with the Stock Exchange' (where the quotations department, for example, already vetted the circulars to shareholders which fly between companies during a take-over bid) was the official description of the policy. 'Fraser and Wareham are there to drag the Stock Exchange into the twentieth century' was how a more jaundiced observer saw it.

Penalties for Breaking the Rules

The dragging did not merely consist in suspending a company's share quotation where the Panel might think it necessary, but equally the issue of sanctions again. The original Bank of England thinking on sanctions was that offenders against the Code would be able to be fined or suspended from their respective associations such as the Stock Exchange or the Issuing Houses Association. But the concept of fines vanished amid the legal problems of whether a 'club' was in any position to fine its members. And the Stock Exchange held out against the form of suspension proposed on the grounds that *its* members alone would bear the brunt of official displeasure—suspension from the Exchange meant a broker would lose his livelihood, suspension from the IHA did not stop a banker, licensed or exempted by the Board of Trade, from carrying on with take-over business.

Although the Code itself was long since ready and the Panel

had been appointed, it took until the end of April 1969 for sanctions to be sorted out. Apart from the usual expressions of the Panel's displeasure, the arrangement agreed on was a compromise and significant in that the voluntary system had begun to be mixed with the legal system. The existing Stock Exchange disciplinary powers against both companies and against their own members was one side of the coin. The other was that the Board of Trade consented to back up the Panel and consider requests to deprive a banker of his livelihood by revoking the exemption of an exempted dealer or the licence of a licensed dealer in securities.

The weak point in the system was that the Panel itself, the arbiter of take-over practice, could only request action and that the Board of Trade or the Stock Exchange could turn down its requests. The strength was that Lord Shawcross, introducing this procedure to the Press, made it clear that the Panel's officials, himself included, would resign if their recommendations were ignored.

As for the Code, it was the subject of much minor rephrasing, a number of relatively minor additions and relatively few major changes in the light of actual bid practice. It is reprinted in full as Appendix IV on page 188. Typical of the rephrasing process, which if anything allowed more not less scope for interpretation, is that of the new Principle 7, in its old form 'Notwithstanding the legal rights of a majority anything done to oppress a minority (in the general and not only the legal sense of the words) is wholly unacceptable.' This has now become: 'Rights of control must be exercised in good faith and the oppression of a minority is wholly unacceptable.'

New Rules of Conduct

Minor additions to the existing rules clarified both principles and practice. Rule 9, for example (covering the duties of directors in control of a company who accepted the lower of two rival offers or rejected a bid altogether, thereby forcing the public shareholders to do the same) used to call on the board to 'be prepared to justify its good faith.' Now the board must 'be prepared to justify its good faith *in the interests of the shareholders as a whole.*'

More practically, Rule 10 called on a board with a controlling shareholding not to transfer control 'unless the buyer undertakes to extend a comparable offer to the remaining shareholders.' Now control should not be transferred 'unless the buyer undertakes to extend *within a reasonable period of time* a comparable offer to the holders of the remaining *equity* share capital, *whether such capital carries voting rights or not*.' Under both Codes Rule 10 applied 'other than in special circumstances'. In neither case are these spelt out; but in the old Code 'in such very exceptional circumstances the Panel should be consulted in advance.' In the new Code 'in such special circumstances the Panel must be consulted in advance *and its consent obtained*.' More important changes of this sort were included on the subject of profit forecasts made by companies in the course of bids, covered under Rule 15. 'Profit forecasts must be compiled by the Directors with the greatest possible care' said the old Code. Says the new:' *Notwithstanding the obvious hazard attached to the forecasting of profits*, profit forecasts must be compiled with the greatest possible care by the Directors *whose sole responsibility they are*.' The old required that the assumptions on which forecasts were based had to be stated in an offer document; the new specifically includes under this heading the *commercial assumptions*. Perhaps the main change under the heading of forecasts was that the reports on them given by auditors or independent accountants and by a company's financial advisers now had to be contained in the offer document sent to shareholders and not merely communicated to the board of directors.

Major changes reflecting recent bid tactics were also incorporated in the Code. Chief of these was that no bid could be made without the Panel's consent unless it was for more than 50 per cent of a company's voting capital, as before, but in a partial bid situation such as Gallaher neither the bidder nor its associates were allowed to deal in the shares of the company during the offer period. In addition, where the Panel agreed to a bid for less than 50 per cent of the capital, bidders and their associates were banned from buying more shares in the company concerned for a full year after the bid had closed.

Bid timing in general was tightened up in the new Code. Under Rule 12 a bidder who declared his intention to make an offer had to produce his formal offer 'within a reasonable time' or be prepared to 'justify the circumstances of the case' to the Panel. Secondly, once an offer was made, it could not be withdrawn during its currency except with the permission of the Panel unless a rival offer had gone unconditional. Thirdly, an overall time limit was imposed—no bid could be declared validly unconditional more than 60 days from the time when the initial offer document was posted. Other minor alterations were made to the various time limits which applied to extensions and re-bids.

The obviously contentious areas of the new Code could arguably be narrowed down to two. The Code still accepted the general belief that 'it is considered undesirable to fetter the market' even if a major proviso, 'save in so far as appears from this Code', had been made. Under the tricky subject of market dealings during the course of a bid, it was again stipulated that general offer terms should be increased to take account of the weighted average prices made in the market: if the terms included stocks and shares, their value was established by reference to the average market price of such stocks and shares during the course of the bid.

There was, however, a let-out: a company could argue that there had been a general change in market prices in the period in question or that new facts had been published which had altered its own market rating, so that the terms of the general offer, supposed to reflect prices paid in market buying, could be varied accordingly. Clearly the scope for argument with the Panel on this subject is tremendous.

Secondly, under the subject of market transactions, the old Code had pointed out that since dealings by associates in the market could frustrate or affect the outcome of a bid, associates were warned that they should be ready to satisfy the Panel that their dealings were not prejudicial to the interests of shareholders. This was a crucial section of the Code and in the News of the World affair it had landed the Panel with a critical decision to make on the role of Hambros and later Morgan Grenfell in effectively blocking Maxwell's bid. Rule 33 of the new Code has done little to cope with the situation except to note that associates in these circumstances are *advised* to consult the Panel in advance and if they do not do so then, as before, to be prepared to justify their actions. The way is still open.

Given fairly radical changes in the staffing of the Panel and in the potential severity of penalties for infringement of the Code, concessions were made to City opinion to establish that the decisions of the Panel were subject to appeal. The appeal committee was to

THE 1969 CITY CODE

be chaired by a former Lord of Appeal, Lord Pearce, and heard by members of the Panel who did not participate in the initial proceedings and did not include the representative of the offender's official City body.

Another protection was that it was made clear that the Panel and its director general did not have any priviledge under the laws of libel in their pronouncements—indeed, Ian Fraser is insured against libel in the sum of £250,000.

In essence, although difficulties remained, the equipment of the new Panel had been remarkably improved. 'However, this can probably all be resolved by a decisive director-general' said a *Times* leading article of the day. 'The few troublesome cases in the past have arisen partly from an insufficient authority and decisiveness at the Panel, stemming from an inevitable lack of experience. The system now proposed can work. It is up to Mr. Fraser.'

7

New Panel's Test of Strength

'Now Wm. Brandt's say that the Take-over Panel will eventually procure a fair price for the company. Now, there are fair prices and fair prices, just as some people are more informed than other people. Can you ask someone to explain why and how the Take-over Panel will get the best price for the company in the end.' Shareholder's question at an extraordinary general meeting of Pergamon Press Ltd., Friday 10 October 1969.

'(In the first six months) something over 22 (offers) presented major problems which the Panel had to consider and on which it has advised, but only 2 of these necessitated formal meetings of the Panel as a whole or attracted the attention of the press.' Lord Shawcross, chairman of The City Panel.

Pergamon Agreement with Leasco

During the struggle for control of News of the World at the beginning of 1969, Mr. Maxwell had put up a profit forecast for Pergamon of £2.5m. before tax. Within months the first accounts of his joint venture in encyclopaedias with the British Printing Corporation could be expected. The joint company, International Learning Systems Corporation, had been formed in the middle of 1967 and ran its first accounting period of eighteen months to the end of December 1968. In the aftermath of the News of the World bid, and in the general stock-market decline of 1969, Pergamon's share price tumbled from 45s. to 25s.

Not many weeks after the new Take-over Panel went to work, Maxwell unveiled his next stock-market deal. It was one to astound the 'bears' of Pergamon Press: on 18 June 1969 at a Press conference at the merchant bank of Rothschilds he revealed that he had agreed to sell out his company to one of the high flyers of the American computer leasing companies, Leasco Data Processing Equipment Corporation. Leasco, headed by 29-year-old Mr. Saul Steinberg, agreed to pay about 37s. a share in a mixture of cash and loan stock convertible into its own common stock, and Maxwell agreed to accept and to procure acceptance by his family interests for a total of not less than 4.3m. Pergamon shares. Since that 4.3m. holding, 1.1m. of which was to accept for cash and the remaining 3.2m. for Leasco loan stock, was 31 per cent of Pergamon's capital, the merger, with Maxwell's blessing, looked certain to succeed.

Pergamon relied for advice on the investment banking house of Robert Fleming, which through the investment trusts it managed held a large number of Pergamon shares: there was no need, it was felt, to call on the services of the big merchant banks like Hill, Samuel, as there had been in the News of the World contest. Leasco, for its part, briefed Rothschilds shortly before the merger terms were made public, treating the matter as a *fait accompli*. Within a couple of weeks, early in July, Leasco demonstated its intentions perfectly plainly; it paid more than £9m. in cash for 2.1m. Pergamon shares in a deal referred to and cleared by the Take-Over Panel. The sellers were mainly the investment trusts managed by Robert Fleming, Maxwell's advisers. It was an expensive demonstration of confidence.

The trouble was that Leasco's confidence was being shaken slowly, though there was no public crack in the façade of amity. The day after the merger terms were made public the American group asked for a detailed breakdown of Maxwell and Maxwell family interests shareholdings in Pergamon. They did not get it. Instead, early in July Maxwell asked for a renegotiation of the terms of his agreement on the grounds that his family interests would not accept the amount of Leasco loan stock (rather than cash) which Maxwell originally pledged them to accept.

Renegotiation began, but there was still no breakdown of shareholdings forthcoming and Leasco had other problems. It had set its accountants, Touche, Ross, Bailey & Smart, to work to sift the Pergamon financial background; but Touche Ross found themselves faced with 'difficulties and delays' in getting the financial information they wanted. The Americans explained later that 'such information had to be given by Mr. Maxwell personally, who naturally was not always readily available.'

Nevertheless, on 28 July 1969 Leasco and Rothschilds received a tentative breakdown of the Maxwell holdings in Pergamon as at 16 July. This showed a total of 4.45m. shares. There was, however, a problem: Pergamon's legal advisers were having trouble confirming some of the holdings. Rothschilds were later informed that a particular family trust with 607,538 shares had transferred its holding into a nominee name. On 4 August a new list followed showing of total of 4.22m. shares and with the information that the family trust in question had already sold 197,203 shares and now held only 410,335 shares.

These were apparently minor difficulties since by 5 August Leasco and Maxwell had agreed new terms; these allowed another 1.1m. of the Maxwell and Maxwell family interests shares, double the original number, to accept cash rather than Leasco loan stock as part of the deal. As a quid pro quo, the Maxwell family interests deposited £2m. to finance Leasco's obligation to deposit funds in the U.K. according to the Exchange Control regulations; and if Maxwell could not persuade his family interests to accept the offer, he was to buy the equivalent number of Pergamon shares in the stock-market if called upon to do so by Leasco.

To round matters off, by 6 August, Leasco's accountants, Touche, Ross, had decided on what particular aspects of Pergamon's financial affairs required further elucidation.

Leasco's Anxieties

At that stage there had been only one slip-up; the sales of Pergamon shares by the foreign-based Maxwell family trust, Bahamas Trustee & Executor, had not been notified to the Take-over Panel as required by the Code's rules on associates dealings, even though sales had started on 10 July. Over the five days between 7 August and 12 August Leasco set out to clarify the problems on Pergamon's profits raised by Touche, Ross. Two specific points were the treatment of profits on property disposals, as opposed to normal publishing and printing earnings, and the much more complex question of profits made by Pergamon on sales of back issues of learned journals to a private family company, Maxwell Scientific International.

According to a subsequent Leasco statement, the trading agreement between the public company, Pergamon, which Leasco was buying, and the private company, Maxwell Scientific International, seemed to be this. At the end of 1967 Pergamon had written down the value of its journal back numbers to nil; in 1968 it sold £660,000 of these back issues to Maxwell Scientific International; since these had been included at no value in the previous Pergamon stock figures, virtually the whole of the £660,000 could be regarded as a Pergamon profit in 1968.

Since then there had been a change in the basis on which Pergamon valued its stock of back numbers and its 1969 profit forecast estimated a profit for Pergamon of £200,000 on sales to Maxwell Scientific International of £670,000. The problem was Pergamon and MSI had an agreement signed in 1967 which could be interpreted as a 'sale or return' contract—what MSI could not sell Pergamon might be called on to take back. At the end of 1968, according to Leasco's information, four-fifths of MSI's journal back numbers were unsold (that is £530,000 worth); and sales by MSI in 1969 were said to be running at approximately the same rate as the year before. If those figures were correct, and if the 1967 agreement was 'sale or return', by the end of 1969 MSI would have more than £1m. worth of unsold journals which it could require Pergamon to take back, making nonsense of Pergamon's projected 1969 profit of £200,000 on the sale of back numbers. Leasco was disturbed at the figuring.

On 12 August 1969 it had something new to worry about. That was the encyclopaedia business, International Learning Systems Corporation, which Pergamon owned jointly with the British Printing Corporation. When negotiations with Maxwell began, Leasco understood that I.L.S.C.'s profits were running at a rate equivalent to about £500,000 a year. Draft accounts for that company's initial trading period to the end of 1968 were made available on 12 August. These showed that in eighteen months I.L.S.C. had enjoyed a devaluation windfall of £346,000 but it had also to provide (from a prior year) £471,000 for insufficient provisions for future bad debts and future interest and collection costs on the instalment debts it was owed; the net result would be a loss for I.L.S.C. of £431,000.

Collapse of the Merger

Obviously Leasco began to wonder how valuable an asset Pergamon's half share of I.L.S.C. might be. There was a further complication. I.L.S.C. had already paid interim dividends of which Pergamon had credited £100,000 to its profit and loss account in 1967 and £108,000 to its reserves in 1968. As Leasco was to put it later, 'the status of these dividends in the absence of profits or reserves of I.L.S.C. out of which to pay them remains to be considered.'

On 14 August Leasco first saw its own advisers Rothschilds and then met Maxwell. The result of that meeting was that Maxwell and his family interests were to receive only half the bid price for their shares, although the rest of the public would still get the full 37s., until Pergamon's forecast profits for 1969 and 1970 were achieved. It was an amazing concession from Maxwell, but one which he withdrew the next day when he discovered that it would have to be publicly disclosed in the offer document sent to all Pergamon's shareholders. Leasco did not give up. On Monday 18 August Saul Steinberg flew into London from New York; and Rothschilds and Flemings, the two companies' merchant banks, spent all day trying to hammer out a retention agreement on the lines to which Maxwell had acquiesced on the 14th. They failed and Flemings were about to reveal that the whole merger was off.

The ensemble, however, was re-formed that night at the home of solicitor and mediator extraordinary, Lord Goodman. In fact between 2 a.m. and 7.30 a.m. on Tuesday the 19th the retention agreement was restored in principle—if Pergamon's profits failed to come up to scratch, Maxwell and his family interests would have the remaining half of the bid price which they had not received trimmed by an amount equal to 15 times the earnings shortfall.

What had not been settled was Leasco's worry over what it had already learnt about Pergamon's profits and I.L.S.C.'s profits. However, into the new scheme with Maxwell was drafted provision for full disclosure on the points that worried the American group and clauses on the accounting principles to be applied in measuring Pergamon's earnings when the scheme had to be put into effect. On the morning of Wednesday 20 August Maxwell objected to this aspect of the draft.

It is incredible that no serious hint of this manoeuvring and crisis had yet reached the public. Pergamon and Leasco, Flemings and Rothschilds, Maxwell and Steinberg had been a long time getting out the formal offer document for what two months earlier had been a willing merger; but Leasco had paid close on £10m. for Pergamon shares in the stock-market and that the merger would go ahead there could be no doubt.

Just as Maxwell and Steinberg were trying to put the pieces together again, however, one journalist, Robert Jones of *The Times*, decided to see whether the Pergamon share register would provide the clues to the delay. Jones, for long a close follower of Pergamon's affairs, knew where to look and quickly found the sort of thing he was looking for. That was share sales by Bahamas Trustee & Executor, one of the Maxwell family trusts, through nominee names into the hands of Leasco-Rothschilds. No such transactions had been published in accordance with the City Code. *The Times* did not publish these facts until its issue of Thursday 21 August, but the previous two days Jones had been asking discreetly around among the interested parties. Rothschilds and Leasco, if not the Take-over Panel, were already aware of the sale of 197,000 shares as we have seen earlier. But the figures Jones had dug out of the share register showed the sales were far larger than that. In the late afternoon of Wednesday 20 August, the day Maxwell had objected to some of the clauses of the new retention agreement with Leasco, Pergamon informed Leasco that not only had Bahamas Trustee & Executor disposed of 197,000 shares of which Rothschilds had been told some weeks earlier, but a further 400,000 had been sold between 10 July and 7 August of which Pergamon had just learnt. For the first time the Take-over Panel was told of these transactions and it went into a hurried session on Wednesday evening.

It had been a trying fortnight of peace and crisis, crisis and peace. For Saul Steinberg the revelation of the full extent of the share sales was simply the last straw. On Thursday the Take-over Panel issued a statement accepting Maxwell's explanations of why the share sales had not been disclosed in accordance with the rules. By the afternoon, however, there was a real crisis to handle. Steinberg had had enough, informed the Panel that he was withdrawing his bid and why, and issued a public statement on the same lines that evening; the same evening the Panel requested that the Stock Exchange suspend Pergamon's share quotation.

Findings of the Panel

In the confused drama that followed, most of it played out in public and therefore well known, the Take-over Panel was faced with one specific and one general problem. Rule 12 of the City Code says that a bidder who has announced his intention to make an offer must proceed with a formal offer within a reasonable time or be prepared to justify the circumstances of the case to the Panel; what is more Leasco had acquired 38 per cent of the Pergamon share capital through the stock-market at 36s. a share and, having thus bought effective control, it was duty bound to pay the same price to all other shareholders even if it did not like what it had subsequently found. (In an almost equally complex case, the fight to gain control of the Beatles song-writing company, Northern Songs, the Panel did eventually demand that ATV follow up its stock-market purchase of shares with a bid to all shareholders, including the company's principal asset, the Beatles themselves). Apart from the particular problem of trying to salvage a bid from Leasco for all other shareholders in Pergamon, the Panel also had to act with a general sense of equity. Leasco's complaints and queries were serious; if the Panel judged them to be fair, could it reasonably require that a bid be made at all?

The recriminations and wild charges that came in the wake of Leasco's withdrawal did nothing to help either side. Maxwell lost his bankers Robert Fleming, themselves at the centre of the controversy having sold the Pergamon shares under their control to Leasco early in the proceedings; Flemings disassociated themselves from some of Maxwell's accusations against Steinberg and Leasco and ceased to act for Pergamon, setting up a hunt throughout the City for new banking advisers to the company. Within a couple of days stockbrokers Panmure Gordon, whose clients had once held 60 per cent of Pergamon's capital, ceased to be brokers to the company. Both Leasco and Pergamon put out long statements to the papers explaining and justifying their positions while working night and day with the Panel to sort out the mess.

When the Panel eventually spoke its collective mind at two o'clock in the morning of 28 August, it was clear that a lot of sorting had been done. There were three main strands in its long and yet terse statement. First, to fulfil its role as the protector of the shareholders of Pergamon Press, the Panel executive had helped to negotiate a completely new merger agreement between Leasco and Pergamon. Regrettably, as it became clear later, the full extent of that agreement, including the question of management, was not immediately made public. What was, was that independent accountants were to be appointed to investigate and establish Pergamon's profits for the years 1968 and 1969 and when that had been done Leasco would make a new bid for all the remaining shares of the company—at 25 times average annual earnings for the general public and only 19 times average annual earnings for the Maxwell interests. It was a bid at an indefinite price at an indefinite time ahead, but as Panel chairman Lord Shawcross put it: 'We have done our best to secure the best interests of outside shareholders.'

Second, however, the Panel broadened its horizons within the general context of Leasco's case, and turned its attention to the specific topics of International Learning Systems Corporation and its profitability and to trading between Pergamon Press and the private company controlled by Maxwell's family interest, Maxwell Scientific International. With a summary of the facts at its disposal, the Panel considered that 'it is a question for further enquiry whether the shareholders of Pergamon received all the information to which they were reasonably entitled about the affairs of I.L.S.C.' and that 'it is certainly for consideration whether there was a proper disclosure of all relevant matters to the shareholders of Pergamon in regard to transactions with Maxwell family interest companies.'

Feeling itself ill-equipped to deal with these wide-ranging accounting and legal questions, the Panel asked the Board of Trade to set up an investigation with the observation that 'having regard to all the circumstances, and not only to the public concern already referred to, the Panel considers that the public interest does require that the true position should be established by an independent investigation. Nothing less will re-establish the position of Pergamon and in the long run protect the interests of its shareholders.'

The public interest seemed a far cry from the voluntary supervision of take-over conduct in the City; and on the technical grounds that the Panel had exceeded its brief Maxwell appealed against its findings. But for the City itself there was a third and even more general shock. The merchant banking community in London both supervises take-over bids and the investment of funds, as Flemings,

Pergamon's advisers and sellers of Pergamon's shares, had done in this particular case.

While Flemings in particular and the City in general successfully reconcile these twin occupations without the slightest suggestion of malpractice, the circumstances of the Pergamon affair decided the Panel to clear the air. 'While the merchant banks concerned in the present matter,' it said, discussed with the Panel administration all relevant purchases or sales and received clearance in regard to them, the Panel contemplates studying the general principles which should apply in circumstances where possible conflicts of interest may be thought to arise in a take-over context.'

Within a couple of weeks of this sweeping set of findings, however, the Panel was called upon to witness and comment on the demise of its hard earned reconciliation between the warring factions. Breakdown this time came on the interpretation of the agreement which the Panel had helped to negotiate and in particular on who was to be the effective chief of Pergamon until the independent accountants had finished their work. Despite mounting opposition from institutional shareholders in his company, despite the fact that the Board of Trade set in train the investigation the Panel had called for and despite the fact that his appeal against the Panel's findings had failed, Mr. Maxwell stuck resolutely to his interpretation of the new agreement. That was that, while he had agreed to resign as managing director of Pergamon in favour of a Leasco nominee, there was no question of the Leasco nominee being day-to-day chief executive of the company. Leasco naturally saw this crucial question differently and so did the Panel. 'It is a matter of regret,' said Ian Fraser, the Panel's director general, 'that Mr. Maxwell has felt unable to accept this interpretation, but in the event the Panel cannot compel parties to carry out an agreement and the matter must be left to the shareholders and to the ordinary processes of law.' What that turned out to mean was the requisitioning of an extraordinary general meeting of Pergamon Press in October 1969 where Leasco, supported by bankers J. Henry Schroder Wagg representing a large block of institutional shareholders, proceeded to vote Robert Maxwell and all his colleagues off the board of Pergamon and to replace them with a new set of directors, in a meeting of pandemonium and occasional farce in which a drove of City lawyers and bankers played leading roles.

8

The Scope of Regulation

'It is important to observe that our system goes much beyond that laid down by the Securities and Exchange Commission in the United States of America. The S.E.C. is primarily concerned with problems of disclosure. The City Panel, of course, deals with these, but it deals also with general problems of conduct arising in the course of merger or take-over transactions.' Lord Shawcross, chairman of the City Panel.

Achievements and Failures

Early in 1970 it is on the handling of the Pergamon Press–Leasco affair that the second City Panel stands to be judged, regardless of its many other interventions into disputed and complex bid arrangements. Pergamon itself remains a continuing story and judgement on the rights and wrongs of the affair itself would be wholly inappropriate. The question is what did the Panel achieve, fail to achieve and how. From the point of view of small shareholders, whose interests it was designed to protect, the Panel's major action has been to prevent the complete collapse of a declared take-over bid which determined the price at which some professional City investors managed to sell their shares. It has managed to maintain the hope of an eventual bid of some sort—albeit a bid in abeyance and one which will almost certainly be lower in value than the 37s. originally offered for each Pergamon share and lower than the 36s. at which many shares were bought by Leasco.

Secondly, it is at the Panel's instigation that two simultaneous enquiries have been launched into the details of Pergamon's profitability and the nature of some of its trading connections, enquiries which, with or without a Leasco bid, should establish for public shareholders a comprehensive picture of their company after considerable City gossip and months of open criticism.

There are, however, more general and more important results. The Panel's questioning of the City on potential conflicts of interest in the merchant banks may not have produced revolutionary results or recommendations, but that it should have been so speedily mounted by a body of this sort is itself a revolution. The last enquiry into such a problem, the Bank Rate tribunal, was greeted with a sense of indignant outrage and produced an interesting study of social life at the top rather than illumination on how the City conducted its affairs.

Undoubtedly the most significant achievement of all is that the method and content of the Pergamon investigation has certainly hastened, if not provoked, the process of accounting reform in Britain, promising something of a long term revolution for industry and finance. The extent and importance of these problems and their potential solutions is, of course, the major topic of this book.

If, on the other hand, the Panel is to be viewed in the light of the City Code itself, then Pergamon–Leasco involved one arguable failure. Having announced a take-over bid and bought Pergamon shares on the basis of that bid price, Leasco was not forced to go through with its offer in strict accordance with the rules. The City can argue with some justice that Leasco is in *de facto* control of Pergamon Press but has been allowed to say that it thinks it made a mistake in its original bid terms and will not carry on with them.

Moreover, when the Panel patched up the differences between Leasco and Robert Maxwell with a detailed and lengthy agreement, it showed itself quite powerless to enforce such an agreement when, in its own view, one of the parties decided not to accept or enact the spirit or terminology of vital clauses.

Operational Philosophy

Both the failures and successes are fundamental to the future regulation of the securities market in London and both in my view reflect the Panel's interpretation of its role and its choice of method and action. Basic to the Panel's present thinking is the opinion that so nebulous a body, isolated halfway between the law and the City's own good intentions, can only be effective by a system dependent on personal contact. The entire Panel staff does not run into double figures. Its chief executives have worked tirelessly and with, on past precedent, great success by constant personal contact with the bankers, lawyers and brokers of the City. The Pergamon affair showed these executives willing to be private negotiators with the accumulated expertise of their banking and Stock Exchange experience. It could be argued that the very closeness of this personal involvement and knowledge of the men in the City is at least a contributory factor to the Panel's failures in being able to enforce its own rules and agreements strictly.

What has been demonstrated is an intelligent desire for natural justice, the wish to establish truth as much as to enforce a take-over bid operating manual. The obvious weakness of this system is the weakness of the previous attempts to keep order in the City. If the merger boom really gets under way again, will the Panel have the time and the opportunity with so small a professional staff to avoid contentious situations slipping through its net? Equally, as a new generation of entrepreneurs make their way in the City, the effectiveness of the closed network is bound to diminish. The rules of the Code and the rulings of the Panel could be made nonsense of by an intelligent financial manipulator unafraid of censure from his co-equals in the City. That the Board of Trade stands behind the Panel has been plainly demonstrated; but effective sanctions remain in the Board of Trade's gift and the willingness with which they are used must inevitably reflect the political attitudes of government.

As long as the voluntary system is to remain, only one failure is required to undermine the resources of the Panel and the disciplinary weapons it holds. This has become, paradoxically, crucially more important in the light of the Panel's achievements in the Pergamon affair, achievements which, admired by the public, depended on the assumption of wide powers not envisaged when the new rules and the new Panel was set up.

The Widening Net of Supervision

When Robert Maxwell appealed against the Panel's findings on the Pergamon–Leasco affair, he did so first and foremost on the ground that, however broadly the Code was interpreted, its rules could only apply to the conduct of companies, their professional advisers and their associates in the course of take-over and merger situations. Clearly the Panel has gone far beyond that and it is worth quoting at some length its observations on the subject together with those of the Panel Appeal Committee. The original Panel statement read:

In the course of its investigations of the circumstances leading to the withdrawal of the proposed Leasco offer, matters came to the notice of the Panel to which, even if the express provisions of the City Code were not attracted, the Panel would feel bound to call attention. These concerned the question whether the Board of Pergamon had properly discharged its obligation to inform its shareholders sufficiently in regard to the affairs of their company.

It must be made clear that the Panel possesses no general supervisory powers to ensure that the directors of public companies make full disclosure to their shareholders of all relevant matters. This is indeed a most important duty of directors and that it should have been continuously discharged becomes a matter of especial importance as soon as any question arises of an offer for shares.

It is for this reason that under its constitution the City Panel's interest in the matter of disclosure is attracted whenever a question arises of a prospective offer, as well as during the course of negotiations about an offer or in the aftermath of an offer which has been made. It may be suggested that the Panel is only concerned with disclosure in the offer document (if indeed one materializes) or in any reply made by the offeree company, but the Panel considers this too narrow a view.

. . . It is not only in offer documents or replies that full disclosure is called for, although it is only in the context of an offer situation that the Panel can draw attention to any inadequacy of disclosure. Observance to the full of this obligation to disclose is essential if public confidence in the securities market is to be maintained.

. . . The Panel considers it of the utmost importance that there should be full and frank disclosure of all relevant circumstances in which transactions take place between a public company and other companies in which a director may have an indirect interest or over which he may be assumed to have some influence whether he has an interest in a technical sense or not.

On Mr. Maxwell's objection to this policy statement the Panel Appeal Committee under Lord Pearce said:

The first point is the contention that the panel strayed beyond its proper sphere. The Panel's statement shows that it was well aware of the fact that its task was to deal with the take-over situation and that a possible view was that it was only concerned with the disclosure in the offer document or in any reply made by the offeree company. But it rejected that view as being too narrow. One of the main objects of the Panel is to secure fair treatment for the investing public. This object can be seen plainly to run through the City Code.

. . . Information given at the time of a bid cannot be wholly divorced from pre-bid information which the shareholder has been given or ought to have been given. The full Panel made a careful investigation as to the take-over situation. The Panel was composed of 11 persons of

standing and experience in the City of London. Their collective knowledge and judgement were very weighty. In their investigation they found a situation which in their opinion called for an inquiry by the Board of Trade in the interests of everybody concerned.
The problem which they consciously faced was whether they should take a narrow view, suppress that opinion as not being their business, and, as it were 'pass by on the other side'. They considered that their duty to the public did not allow them to take that course. They, therefore, expressed the opinion they had formed. In the particular circumstances of every case it must be a question of fact and degree whether such an expression of opinion is justifiable. In this the importance of the suggested non-disclosure and its relevance to the existing and future situation of the company would be factors to be considered. That question of fact and degree must be decided in the light of fairness and commonsense. That decision in this case was made by men whose knowledge of the City made them particularly suitable to form such a judgement. We think that the course taken by the full Panel was reasonable in the circumstances and we see no reason to differ from it.

The Weakness of Divided Authority

The Panel findings on the Pergamon Press–Leasco case, and the decision of the Appeals Committee, display a general desire for the protection of shareholders of, and indirectly the employees and creditors of, public companies. It is not surprising that the interests of the public do not always coincide with the interests of company directors and their professional financial advisers, and confidence in the financial system can only survive if such conflicting interests are seen to be reconciled by independent authority. This, as the Appeals Committee pointed out, is the philosophy that runs through the City Code.

It is also the philosophy reflected in the Panel's action—the launching of enquiries into Pergamon Press and City conflicts of interest, the calls for reform of accounting procedure in Britain, the detailed examination of the existing Companies Acts and the Stock Exchange rules for the quotation of securities. It is the basis of the financial system that is under scrutiny.

This is not merely the unfounded assertion of a group of men with a desire to interfere widely in the conduct of business. The value of the Pergamon–Leasco affair is that such detailed exposure has demonstrated that particular problems of shareholder protection and the rational conduct of the securities market cannot be solved without fundamental reform covering an extensive range of professional behaviour. The Panel interpretation of its own role has been that it is duty bound to be the agent of such reform.

Simultaneously, however, it has, willingly or otherwise, faced the logical difficulty that this is a process which the Panel can barely start and certainly not supervise or finish. The action taken as a result of Pergamon–Leasco was only possible in the context of a bid situation and the Appeals Committee made it clear that a bid situation in itself is not enough to justify such enquiries. 'It must be a question' said the Appeals Committee, 'of fact and degree whether such opinion is justifiable', thereby leaving the propriety of the Panel's investigatory decisions always open to contention.

Even when the Panel can get started, however, it remains doubtful whether it has the authority to direct government on companies legislation, bankers on banking, accountants on accounting, and the Stock Exchange on control of the stock-market. The Panel's staff, though professional, is small, its disciplinary powers are dependent on the consent of others, and it remains the shadowy creature of the Bank of England. At the present time, on severely restricted occasions, all it can give is advice. It can take decisions in the limited context of specific take-over dealings, but even then its opinions are subject to the laws of libel.

The Panel has demonstrated, if the proposition needed further demonstration, that if shareholders are to be protected, a body with equal vigour, but greater power and a wider brief, is needed in the City to act both as an agent of reform and occasionally as a policeman. The history of take-over regulation has shown that the City and its satellite professions have conspicuously failed to initiate the necessary changes or to exercise the required supervision. What remains to be devised is not an authoritative City Panel on Takeovers and Mergers, but an authoritative City Panel.

Part Two

Reforming Accounting Principles

by
Edward Stamp

NOTE

It is emphasised that none of the statements or references in Part Two of this book is intended as a reflection on the integrity or professional competence of any public accounting firm in Britain or the United States. It is the quality and adequacy of 'accounting principles' that is in question, along with the form of the relationship beween auditors and their 'clients'.

Professor Stamp has made this point explicitly on several occasions. See, for example, the reports in *Accountancy* (December 1969, p. 987) and in *The Accountant* (15 November 1969, pp. 666–667) of his speech to the Manchester Society of Chartered Accountants on 30 October 1969; and his letter to the *Financial Times*, published on 25 November 1969.

9

A Crisis in the Accounting Profession

Accountants are generally regarded as rather dull and uninteresting people. The case was put very well by the American humourist H. L. Mencken, many years ago:

> Suppose you had your free choice between going to a convention of Rotarians and going to a convention of accountants, which would you choose? Obviously you would choose the convention of Rotarians, just as you would go to the Folies Bergere rather than to a meeting of the Ladies' Aid Society. Accountants, in their way, are the wisest of men. Once, working as a newspaper reporter, I covered one of their assemblages, and in four days I didn't hear a single foolish word. What they said was sober, sound and indubitable. But it was also as flat as dishwater.

Many people doubtless feel that the nature of the accountant's work is so tediously unimaginative that the man's personality is shaped and indeed warped by it. This certainly seems to be the view held by many novelists and movie and television scriptwriters. The work of the auditor is probably regarded as the most soul-destroying of all. Thus, Elbert Hubbard, another American writer, described the auditor in the following terms:

> The typical auditor is a man past middle age, spare, wrinkled, intelligent, cold, passive, non-committal, with eyes like a codfish; polite in contact, but at the same time unresponsive, calm and damnably composed as a concrete post or a plaster of Paris cast; a petrifaction with a heart of feldspar and without charm of the friendly germ, minus bowels, passion or a sense of humour. Happily they never reproduce and all of them finally go to Hell.

These are American expressions of opinion, but it is doubtful if British accountants have any more exciting an image. To say that a man has 'the mind of a chartered accountant' is to characterise him as a person who is intelligent, reliable and honest; and who is also inclined to be dull, unimaginative and slightly pompous.

Yet it is doubtful whether a reputation for dullness, lack of imagination, or even pomposity, has unduly troubled accountants on either side of the Atlantic, or indeed anywhere else in the world. In fact the accountant in public practice (who does the auditing) is much more concerned with the reputation he has earned for competence and integrity. If this has had to be achieved at the cost of seeming to be a bit of a bore, then so be it; it is a small price to pay for the benefits of practising such a lucrative profession.

This, until recently, has been about the sum and substance of the accountant's public relations problems. All he has had to cope with, if he cared about it at all, was a reputation for being a pretty dull, pencil-pushing stick-in-the-mud.

But not any more. The investing public is now much more inclined to hold accountants responsible for the demonstrated weaknesses of accounting, and some accountants have bleated that they are being treated as scapegoats. Many of the accountants' sacred cows (and even some of their sacred bulls) have been marched off to the slaughter-house; few of them seem likely to survive. Many of their most cherished shibboleths, even including the belief in their judgement, are being questioned, and the profession faces a crisis of confidence which it would be foolish to ignore.

Criticism in America

A lot of the questions which are now exercising the profession, and the public at large, have been debated privately for many years in academic circles and in the higher intellectual reaches of the profession. One of the first indications that the problems were breaking out into the public arena came in November and December 1960, with the publication in *Fortune* of the article 'The Auditors have arrived'. Although this article was generally quite complimentary, it revealed the existence of an acrimonious debate which had been going on for several years within the American profession on the question of the determination of accounting principles. Leading the dissident anti-establishment forces, and very much in a minority, was the senior partner of one of the largest public accounting firms in the world, Leonard Spacek of Arthur Andersen & Co.

Spacek may still be in a minority, but it is a very much larger minority today than it was ten years ago. In the interval the investing public in the United States has become much better aware of the shortcomings in 'generally accepted accounting principles' and this awareness, along with pressure from the Securities and Exchange Commission, and from Leonard Spacek and his allies, has forced the American Institute of Certified Public Accountants into a vast programme of reform. A recent article, in the June 1968 issue of *Fortune,* entitled 'The Accountants are changing the rules' makes it clear how much ground has been covered since 1960.

Indeed, in the last ten years American accountants have been subjected to a rising chorus of criticism from the American financial press. In an article in the 15 May 1967 issue of *Forbes* magazine (a leading American financial journal) entitled 'What are Earnings? The Growing Credibility Gap', one of the partners of Peat, Marwick, Mitchell & Co., the largest public accounting firm in the United States, is quoted as saying 'We have the gun at our back today'. As the *Forbes* article states

Now all at once there are more than fifty major lawsuits pending against the Big Eight public accounting firms which handle about 80% of the U.S. auditing business of listed companies, charging irregularities and negligence in preparing earnings reports and other financial statements. Not the least of these is the suit against Peat, Marwick, Mitchell & Co. in the celebrated Yale Express bankruptcy case. In 1965 it was suddenly discovered that the company's very healthy profits for 1963 and 1964 were in fact losses.[1]

One of the important contributing factors to this chaotic state of affairs has been the fact that 'accounting principles' offer company management the choice of so many different ways of reporting similar transactions that it has become very difficult to know exactly what the accountant means when he talks about, for example, 'profit'. This whole question will be dealt with in more detail in Chapter 10, but in the meantime it is interesting to look at another example quoted by *Forbes*.

Forbes described this as 'the classic case in which the auditors were talked into stretching accounting methods'. The case involved the sale of the shares of Ethyl Corporation by its joint owners, General Motors Corporation and Standard Oil Company of New Jersey. Each owned 50 per cent of Ethyl's shares, and each had held

---

[1] The whole article is reprinted in Keller & Zeff, *Financial Accounting Theory II* (New York: McGraw-Hill, 1969) pp. 5–18. This extract is on p. 5.

them for 38 years, and each would net approximately 40 million dollars on the sale. But, as *Forbes* said, 'when Jersey and G.M. stockholders opened their annual reports a few months later, the deal could not have looked more different'. General Motors had recorded the proceeds as income for the year, before even a penny of operating expenses had been deducted. Standard Oil of New Jersey had gone to the other extreme and had not shown the Ethyl profit in its earnings statement at all but had 'buried it' in the 'Statement of Stockholders' Equity'. *Forbes* went on to say

The contrast was spectacular. Here were the two largest industrial corporations in the world, with over 2 million stockholders and most of the financial community looking on. Yet each came up with a radically different treatment of earnings from the identical transaction. What's more, the treatments had been duly certified by two of the nation's most respected accounting firms, Haskins & Sells [international affiliates of Deloitte, Plender & Griffiths & Co.] for G.M., and Price Waterhouse for Jersey.

The accountants have never made any claims that theirs is an exact trade. In fact, until the recent uproar developed, they never said anything at all, and that may have been an even greater sin. By silently hiding behind their congressionally ordained image of independence they caused, perhaps unintentionally, many people to believe that accounting and earnings figures were something they were not. Admits Walter Hanson, the managing partner of Peat, Marwick, Mitchell: 'Quite frankly, we found that it was to our advantage not to destroy people's illusions about us'.

But the illusions have been shattered anyway. . . .[2]

It would be pleasant to be able to think that the rest of the accounting world, including Britain, could sit back and comfortably ignore what has been taking place in the United States. Unfortunately, accounting 'principles' are pretty much the same the whole world over, and the British variety has no claim to superiority. British accountants and British business men may have higher moral standards than their American opposite numbers (although we should try not to be too smug about this) but when the basic principles are at fault it seems inevitable that the American pattern of public discontent with the profession will be repeated here.

Criticism in Britain

There is a growing amount of evidence to indicate that this is exactly what is happening. The quality of the accounting informa-

---
[2] ibid. pp. 12-13.

tion presented to shareholders was called into question in 1966 during the investigation into the difficulties experienced by Pye. A commentator in *Accountancy* (the official journal of the Institute of Chartered Accountants in England and Wales) observed that 'all told the total amount lost or written off by the Group to 31 March 1966 came to over £9 million. The accounts do not show this total; it is necessary to look in six or more places to make up the figure'.[3]

This perhaps could be written off as a minor eccentricity. But there were growing signs that leading members of the business community were getting fed up with the apparently haphazard approach of British accountants. In June 1968 a good deal of publicity was given to a statement by Sir Frank Kearton, F.R.S., (Chairman of Courtaulds, and Chairman of the Industrial Reorganisation Corporation from 1966 to 1968)[4] saying that he had written to the President of the English Institute to complain about the plethora of generally accepted accounting principles. Sir Frank was very concerned about the difficulties this caused in trying to reconcile pre- and post-acquisition 'principles' in take-overs. The complaint was quietly smothered by the Institute, and nothing was done to cure the problem.

The following month the same problem erupted elsewhere. The previous October (1967), A.E.I. had been fighting a take-over bid from G.E.C., and the A.E.I. directors had announced (in the *tenth* month of 1967) that their profit forecast for 1967 was £10 million (before tax). A major accounting firm reviewed the forecasts on behalf of Baring Brothers (the financial advisers to A.E.I.) and declared that on the basis of the enquiries they had made the forecasts for 1967, 1968 and 1969 had in their view 'been prepared on a fair and reasonable basis and in a manner consistent with the principles followed (by A.E.I.) in preparing recent published annual accounts.'

G.E.C. were successful in their take-over bid, and in July 1968 it was announced that A.E.I. had suffered a loss of £4½ million in 1967! Of the shortfall of £14½ million it was stated that £5 million was attributed 'to matters substantially of fact' whilst the

---

[3] *Accountancy*, December 1966, p. 883.
[4] Sir Frank was made a life peer in the 1970 New Year's Honours List.

remaining £9½ million was due to 'adjustments which remain matters substantially of judgement'.

One of the most unsatisfactory features of the whole affair was the fact that not even the former directors of A.E.I. were able to get full disclosure of what the differences were all about.[5] The shrouds of secrecy contrasted strangely with the welter of disclosure the previous October when the protagonists were vying with each other for the shareholders' votes.

More recently, and perhaps the most important so far as its effect on the general complacency of the accounting profession is concerned, there has been the Pergamon affair. If there is any truth in the adage 'it's an ill wind that blows nobody any good' we may perhaps hope that the disclosures made in the Autumn of 1969, during the course of this take-over battle, have finally stirred the British accounting profession into action. However since some of the allegations on accounting matters made in the *Sunday Times* have resulted in writs being issued by the accountants concerned, no further detailed comment is possible here.

Nevertheless the very fact that at least four different large and highly respectable firms of public accountants have been called in at one time or another to check and re-check what has been going on, and the fact that the Board of Trade agreed to make an investigation to determine whether or not the Pergamon shareholders had been given all the information they required, led to quick and critical reactions in the quality Press. This must surely be cause for great concern amongst thinking accountants.

Thus in the 22 October 1969 issue of *The Guardian* an article by a City journalist entitled 'Auditors under a Cloud' observed that 'on two separate occasions recently the accuracy of auditors' reports has been questioned in public. This is obviously a highly unsatisfactory situation, and unless steps are taken to restore faith in our auditing firms by ensuring that they really do act as shareholders' watchdogs, a major row will break which will do the accounting profession lasting damage'. The article continues,

The standing of Britain's auditing firms has never been at a lower ebb. For years now there has been a growing unease that auditors are too ready to follow blindly the instructions of a Board in respect of such

---

[5] See Sir Joseph Latham, *Take-Over, The facts and the myths of the GEC-AEI battle* (London: Iliffe, 1969) pp. 54–56.

factors as depreciation policy and stock valuation without facing squarely the question of whether the methods are the right ones for proper conduct of the business and the protection of shareholders' interests.
But now the problem has taken a more serious turn with the accuracy of auditors' reports publicly questioned in two highly publicised cases. Counsel for John Bloom in the Rolls Razor case attempted in court to lay part of the blame for the failure of the company on the auditors and claimed that his client had been seriously misled. He was only prevented from making his case fully because the Judge ruled that it was irrelevant to the trial.
And in the hard fought battle over Pergamon Press the auditors have not escaped the backwash. The Board of Trade has ruled that there is a *prima facie* case for an investigation into the affairs of the company, which has an unblemished record so far as one can tell from the auditor's reports.

The article goes on to say that although 'auditors have always tended to adopt too complacent a view' they are going to be drawn into the limelight a lot more whether they like it or not.

The Economist, in its issue of 30 August 1969, also commented on the accounting implications of the Pergamon affair. They observed that,

Accountants do not have, nor do they believe in, written rules. Apart from the information and method of presentation required by the Companies Act, they rely on integrity and common sense, guided by occasional statements issued by the various professional institutions. These carry none of the legal weight that similar recommendations from institutions of American accountants do. They merely represent the evolving concept of what constitutes 'best practice', and the need to define this only arises when accountants find themselves increasingly meeting situations that defeat their common sense.

The Economist concluded its article:

A blow up on this scale is mercifully rare. But when it happens it reveals dangerously hit-and-miss methods by which company accounts get audited by accountants who are often understaffed, working against pressure of time, facing possibly hostile and strong-minded directors and with too much left to individual discretion. Playing the game is all very well and most accountants do. But the system which has been exposed so lamentably this week in the City's handling of this mess-up simply is not good enough.

The general remarks do not of course imply any reflections on the professional integrity of accountants. But they support the case for reform, though not necessarily along the lines advocated by *The Economist* that accounting rules should be written into the Companies Act. This will be commented upon later.

English Institute under Fire

Another article which gave rise to a considerable amount of apoplexy in the profession (and, fortunately, to some more constructive reactions), entitled 'Auditing the Auditors', written by myself, appeared in the 11 September issue of *The Times*. Indeed, the implications of this article were thought to be so serious by the Institute of Chartered Accountants in England and Wales[6] that their President, Mr. R. G. Leach (senior partner in the London office of Peat, Marwick, Mitchell & Co., and one of the inspectors appointed by the Board of Trade to look into the Pergamon affair), wrote a reply which was published in *The Times* on 22 September 1969. My article, Mr. Leach's reply, and my rejoinder are reproduced in Appendix I. My article in *The Times* was a brief condensation of views which I had expressed at much greater length several months previously in an article entitled 'The Public Accountant and the Public Interest', published in *The Journal of Business Finance* in the Spring of 1969. This is reproduced in Appendix III. Readers who are interested in an operational definition of the phrase 'to present a true and fair view', as given by *Accountancy,* the official journal of the English Institute, should study the material in Appendix II.

On 10 November 1969 the *Financial Times* published an article entitled 'The trouble with accountants', based on interviews with several members of the English Institute's Council. Although it was mildly critical, by comparison with what had gone before it read like a paeon of praise. It was hailed by *The Accountant* as 'an honest endeavour to get to grips with the fundamentals of the subject . . . presenting the nearest approach to a realistic view we have yet seen by an outsider' (15 November, 1969, p. 636). Unfortunately, the article produced a spate of correspondence, critical of accountants, which only served to underline the complaints which had been aired elsewhere.

Later the same month, at a meeting on 20 November, in Manchester, Lord Shawcross (Chairman of the City Panel on Take-overs and Mergers) commented on the fact that so many different accounting judgements of the same situation seemed possible. This, he said, could lead to different figures being put forward by the accountants acting for one company from those put forward by

---

[6] Hereinafter referred to as 'the English Institute'.

accountants acting for the other. It could cause 'confusion, adverse comment and anxiety'. Lord Shawcross suggested it might be as well 'if the (English) Institute were perhaps to define more clearly what was the correct practice which had to be followed by all accountants in matters of this kind'.

Thus by December 1969 it had become clear to the English Institute that something had to be done to meet the criticisms being so widely voiced. On 11 December the Institute called a press conference to announce their 'Statement of Intent' to seek improvements. This declaration is commented upon in Chapter 15.

Whatever the Institute does in the future it is essential that it be guided by a determination to develop accounting principles which will produce financial accounts which are relevant to the needs of investors, particularly of small investors. In my view the test of the quality of accounting principles and disclosure requirements in the 1970s must be: are they adequate to enable small investors to form a realistic view of the value of a company's shares? This, as we shall see in the next chapter, is not regarded as an objective of the Institute's present body of 'Recommendations on Accounting Principles.' Such an attitude is not good enough, and the Institute must consider who suffers if their remedies are poorly conceived. As *The Economist* stated, in the article from which we have already quoted,

The conclusion must be that major companies, provided the calibre of their advice is good enough, are not necessarily put at a disadvantage by the possibility that profit forecasts may contain a wide margin of error and accounts a large measure—to be charitable—of eccentricity. They can usually form their own very good idea of a company's worth, even when they have no figures to go on. And so can some of the big institutional investors: witness the trusts that have sold their Pergamon shares. The people who are at a disadvantage are, as usual, the small, the not too well briefed, and the not quite on the ball. And it is these people that the accountancy profession must seriously consider how it is going to protect. About 30 per cent of Pergamon's shares are still held by people who could still lose quite substantial sums out of this take-over bid because (a) they were not sharp enough to sell out in time and (b) they did not have enough information about the state of the Pergamon business.

10

Accounting Principles: The Challenge

In order to see to what extent the accounting profession is taking care of the interests of the small investor we must turn to the question of accounting principles: what are they and how are they determined.

Economics is a discipline closely allied to accountancy. Economic science, particularly in the field of micro-economics, tackles many of the problems which are also dealt with by the accountant. Most economists however, whilst agreeing that their own subject is built upon a well-constructed foundation of principles, would seriously question whether the same could be said about accountancy. And this opinion would undoubtedly be shared by many accountants.

The Nature of Financial Accounts

In order to explain how this has come about, and what it means to the investor, we must first of all consider the end products of the accounting process, namely the financial statements or reports which the accountant produces for the information and use of management, investors, and others to assist them in the process of decision-making. These financial reports include the Balance Sheet, the Statement of Profit & Loss (or 'Income Statement'), the Profit & Loss Appropriation Account (or 'Statement of Retained Earnings'), and (frequently in North America and to some extent in the United Kingdom) a Statement of Source and Application of Funds.

Let us consider briefly what these statements are intended to represent.

A *Balance Sheet* is a statement of financial position at a particular point of time. It consists essentially of a listing of all the assets (classified into significant groups such as cash, debtors, stocks, land, buildings, etc.) which have been acquired by the enterprise as a result of transactions; a list of all the liabilities incurred (also classified into significant categories); and an analysis of the difference between the value of the assets and the value of the liabilities, which is the proprietor's or shareholder's interest. This residual interest will consist of, amongst other things, subscribed capital, and retained profits.

Three things should be noticed immediately. In the first place the assets include only those assets, tangible and otherwise, which have been acquired in transactions. Many other assets, commonly subsumed under the general heading of 'Goodwill', are omitted altogether from the Balance Sheet.

In the second place it should be borne in mind that nothing has yet been said about the basis used to *value* the assets. It is when we come to the question of valuation that some of the greatest weaknesses in modern accounting practice are revealed.

Thirdly, it should be realised that the Balance Sheet is a statement of *position* at a *point in time*. By itself it is therefore of little value in assessing the worth of an enterprise, since it tells us very little about the progress which has been made by the enterprise. An investor with only a Balance Sheet to work from is rather like a ship's navigator who knows the ship's position but who has no idea of its speed or the direction in which it is travelling. The investor, like the navigator, would find it very difficult to make any sensible predictions about the future. In a crude sense, a Balance Sheet is rather like a still picture taken from a movie film. In order to be up to date on what has happened we also need to know what has gone on between one still (or Balance Sheet) and the next. This is where the Statement of Profit and Loss and the Statement of Source and Application of Funds come in.

The *Statement of Profit & Loss* is a representation of the financial progress made by the enterprise over a period of time, generally the period of time that has elapsed since the date of the last Balance Sheet. It shows the revenues which have been earned in that period of time, the expenses which have been incurred, and the resultant profit or loss.

The *Statement of Retained Profits* is also a 'period' rather than a 'position' statement. It will normally show the amount of the retained profits at the beginning of the accounting period, the amount by which they have been increased (decreased) during the period by the profits (losses) earned within the period, any decreases resulting from dividends paid, and the resultant balance of retained profits at the end of the accounting period. However, as we shall see later, several other items may also creep into this statement from time to time.

These three statements between them can tell an investor much of what he wants to know. In many cases, particularly in large companies, he will also need the *Statement of Source and Application of Funds,* which supplies information about the often complex movements of working capital into and out of the business in the accounting period.

However, whether the investor has three or four statements to look at, the value that he can get from them is limited by the assumptions made by the accountant who drew up the statements, and the conventions, rules, even perhaps the 'principles', which he used in arriving at his valuations or measurements.

The Inutility of British Accounts

It is here that we run headlong into the problem of accounting principles. The task of defining and codifying accounting principles in this country has been left pretty much in the hands of the professional accounting bodies. One of them, the English Institute, has published a series of Recommendations on Accounting Principles. In the recommendation (N15) dealing with 'Accounting in relation to changes in the purchasing power of money' which was issued in May 1952, the Council of the Institute had the following observations to make on the nature and purpose of 'accounts' (i.e. the financial statements we have been discussing above).

The Council cannot emphasise too strongly that the signficance of accounts prepared on the basis of historical cost is subject to limitations, not the least of which is that the monetary unit in which the accounts are prepared is not a stable unit of measurement. In consequence the results shown by accounts prepared on the basis of historical cost are not a measure of increase or decrease in wealth in terms of purchasing power; nor do the results necessarily represent the amount which can prudently be regarded as available for distribution, having regard to the financial requirements of the business. Similarly the results shown by such accounts are not necessarily suitable for purposes such as price-fixing, wage negotiations and taxation, unless in using them for these purposes due regard is paid to the amount of profit which has been retained in the business for its maintenance.

This, as Professor David Solomons said, 'seems pretty much to throw away the baby with the bathwater'.[1]

Some people might be forgiven for thinking that the bath-tub has been thrown out as well, because in a much later statement, issued in August 1965, discussing the liability of accountants to third parties, the Institute states,

> No claim by an individual shareholder, however, would succeed in respect of loss suffered through his own investment decisions made on the strength of misleading company accounts supported by an auditors' report containing negligent misrepresentations, since the purpose for which annual accounts are normally prepared is not to enable individual shareholders to take investment decisions.[2]

The small investor, to whose interests this book is principally directed, may be rather surprised to learn that the English Institute takes such a cavalier attitude towards his problems. The situation will become more understandable, perhaps, if we go back about fifty years, into an age in which many accountants still seem to be living.

'Stewardship' Accounting [3]

It is only relatively recently that the needs of the smaller investor have been recognised by professional accountants, and it is only really in North America where they are yet being seriously catered to. Many accountants, even today, regard financial accounts as being simply reports on stewardship. That is to say, the accounts are merely intended to report the sources of the funds which have been invested by the Directors and the manner in which the Directors have invested these funds. This is still a reasonable approach in the case of trustee accounts, but it is scarcely relevant to the needs of the modern investor.

One can appreciate how slowly the needs of the investor (particularly the small investor) have been recognised if one looks briefly

---

[1] See David Solomons, 'Economic and Accounting Concepts of Income', *The Accounting Review*, Vol. XXXVI., No. 3 (July 1961) (pp. 374-383) at p. 383.
[2] Statement S8 (Accountants' Liability to Third Parties), paragraph 8(b).
[3] The term 'stewardship' is employed here in the sense in which it was used in the past. In their publication, *Companies Legislation in the 1970s*, the English Institute (and three other U.K. accounting bodies) use it to denote companies whose ownership is divorced from management (as distinct from 'proprietary' companies where the management also owns control).

at the history of the Companies legislation. The 1900 Companies Act required that the auditors report on 'accounts examined by them and every balance sheet laid before the company in general meeting'; there was no reference to a statement of profit and loss and the general feeling at that time was that profits, and especially such components of profits as sales, were secrets which should not be disclosed to shareholders. It was not until 1967 that British companies were required to disclose sales, although such disclosure has been required by the SEC in the United States for many years.

In the report of the 1906 Company Law Amendment Committee (The Warmington Committee) it was recommended in relation to the balance sheet that it should be 'examined and reported on by the company's auditors. We do not intend that such a balance sheet should include (*sic*) a statement of profit and loss. Although it has been objected that filing such a balance sheet would be detrimental to the company by giving some information as to their profits, and so stimulating competition (*sic*), we consider that such a balance sheet should be filed annually'. It was not until the 1928 Amendment that the Act required directors 'once at least in every calendar year to lay before the company in general meeting a profit and loss account'. It was not until 1947 that the auditor's report was required to bring the profit and loss account within its purview.[4]

The stewardship approach to the preparation of accounts developed in an age when there was little divorce (as there is today) between ownership and management. They were both 'insiders', as they still are today in many private companies. The outsiders were mainly lenders, and they were supplied with accounts which concentrated on giving information about liquidity rather than earning capacity. It is only relatively recently (more recently in Britain than in North America) that managers have had to consider the information needs of a large group of outside equity holders—the small shareholders.

Accounting Principles: the Conventional Wisdom

If one thinks of the needs of creditors in days gone by, bankers and mortgagees, with their preoccupation with questions of security,

---

[4] See Leonard W. Hein, 'The Auditor and the British Companies Acts', *The Accounting Review*, Vol. XXXVIII., No. 3 (July 1963) (pp. 508–520) pp. 517–518.

realisability and liquidity, it becomes easier to understand how the corpus of accounting principles, which are still regarded as relevant today by many accountants, was first developed. The more important of these so-called principles, doctrines, or rules, can be summarised as follows:

Conservatism. This doctrine, which is one of the antecedents of the lower of cost or market rule in stock valuation, is concerned essentially with asset valuation and recognition of income. If there is doubt about the value of an asset it is conservative to value it as low as possible; if there is doubt about whether revenue has been earned then it is conservative to defer recognition of the revenue; if there is doubt about the amount at which a liability should be stated then it is conservative to use the higher valuation. Clearly such a doctrine is in the interests of lenders since they are much less likely to suffer loss if they rely on financial statements which are conservative and if it subsequently turns out that errors existed.

Realisation. The realisation convention requires that revenues and profits shall not be recognised until they have been realised. Thus suppose a company owns some shares in Courtaulds which have tripled in value since they were purchased at a cost of £1,000. It would be wrong, under the realisation convention, to give any recognition in the accounts to the 'paper profit' of £2,000. This rule applies to all assets, and it is really the obverse of the 'historical cost' principle, which states that assets must be recorded at the amounts which they cost the enterprise, regardless of any value increases which may have taken place since then. (However, the doctrine of conservatism requires that losses in value should be recognised by writing down the value of the assets.)

Objectivity. Essentially, this principle requires that valuations shall be made only on the basis of evidence which is independently verifiable. Auditors in particular are seduced by the force of this 'principle', and this is one reason why the accounting profession has stuck so grimly to historical costs through long periods of inflation. They remain committed to historical costs partly because they believe firmly that the recognition of unrealised value differences above (but not below) historical cost would mean a violation of the objectivity principle. In fact, as many accountants ought to know but apparently do not, even the historical cost principle leaves a great deal to be desired from the standpoint of objectivity.[5] Objectivity is of considerable importance as a criterion in evaluating accounting evidence, but most accountants would admit that since so much of their work has to be based upon estimates, it is impossible to be wholly objective about the valuation of any asset, except possibly cash. One surely needs to consider whether objectivity is so important that it should override the need for *relevant* information.

Consistency. The doctrine of consistency states, essentially, that once having adopted a rule of valuation, income measurement, etc. in preparing accounts one is required to follow it consistently from one year to another. The Companies Act requires departures from consistency to be disclosed along with the monetary value of their effect. The existence of this principle represents a tacit acceptance by accountants of the fact that many of their rules are arbitrary, and that in many cases there are several different rules all equally appropriate to the handling of a given situation in the accounts. As soon as one is faced with a multiplicity of more or less arbitrary rules covering similar types of situation one is driven inevitably into enunciation of a consistency principle. Unfortunately, if several similar enterprises end up choosing different accounting rules to measure the same things, and if they are consistent year by year in applying the rules, then it becomes very difficult to compare the position and the progress of the several enterprises. In such cases there is loss of comparability, and there is no doubt that the investor suffers as a result.

The previous four principles have, one way and another, held back the development of accounting theory; consequently they have also impeded the reports which would be relevant to the needs of contemporary users. There are, however, two other 'principles' that have been developed over the last several generations which *are* of value, and which should be retained, more or less intact, in the future. These are:

Full disclosure. This principle requires that a set of accounts must disclose all of the relevant information which the reader requires in order not to be misled. Accountants unfortunately only pay lip service to this rule in many cases. To take just one example, very

---

[5] See, for example, pp. 119–120 of Backer (ed.), *Modern Accounting Theory*, (Englewood Cliffs: Prentice-Hall, 1966)

few companies (Philips, the Dutch electrical firm, is a conspicuous exception) make any attempt to disclose current valuations of all of their assets. Since historical costs are seldom relevant to the needs of investors it is clear that the full disclosure principle is being violated by most companies, or perhaps one should say that it is being consistently overridden by the historical cost principle.

Materiality. This is really a subsidiary principle which qualifies the application of the full disclosure principle. It states in effect that it is only necessary, in cases of doubt, to disclose items which are 'material'. In a sense this begs the question, since one has to define 'material'. The question can be begged further by defining a material item as one the failure to disclose which would render the accounts misleading. The Canadian Institute of Chartered Accountants, and more recently the English Institute, have published statements dealing with this problem. One should hasten to add that failure to disclose current values can scarcely be justified on grounds that they are not material!

The first four principles served accountants well in the days when accounts were regarded principally as reports on stewardship and mainly of interest (so far as the outsider was concerned) to large creditors. The rules were also quite satisfactory in assisting management in the determination of dividend policy, and in deciding whether payment of a dividend would contravene the legal rules governing dividend payments. Since the war however, first in America and more recently in this country, the needs of the smaller outside investor have become more and more important. In addition, the pace of technological improvement and the growing sophistication of the securities markets (to name but two of the many factors involved) have resulted in business enterprises becoming steadily more complex, and more difficult to manage and control. The increasing complexity of the transactions which accountants are called upon to handle has provided further difficulties for the profession. The problems seem to be increasing at an accelerating rate, and any British accountants who feel complacent about the situation need only look at what is happening today in America to get some idea of what is likely to face us in this country in ten years' time.

The Proliferation of New Rules and Procedures

Accountants were initially rather poorly armed and equipped to deal with the new requirements and the new problems. The stone age weapons of conservatism, historical cost, and consistency, were scarcely adequate to deal with the situation that has developed since World War II. Accountants, particularly British accountants, have adapted to the changing circumstances by adopting the pragmatic approach of manufacturing new rules as they seemed required to meet new circumstances. Fires have been put out as they started but, except until recently in America, little if any attention has been paid to fire prevention.

The problem has been compounded by the fact that it has become generally accepted in the profession and in the business community that the full responsibility for the selection of the particular accounting principles or rules to be used in preparing a company's accounts rests on the management and the directors. The auditor's responsibility consists in making whatever examination he believes to be necessary of the accounts, and the underlying records, in order to form and express an opinion as to whether or not the accounts present 'a true and fair view' of the company's financial position and progress. In its statement on 'General principles of auditing' the English Institute deals with this matter as follows:

> Responsibility for the accounts and financial control of a company rests upon the directors. Their statutory duties include responsibility for ensuring the maintenance of adequate records and the preparation of annual accounts showing the true and fair view required by the Act. They are responsible for safeguarding the assets of the company and are not entitled to rely upon the auditors to protect them from any shortcomings in carrying out their responsibilities.
>
> Auditors have their own independent responsibility to form and express their professional opinion on the accounts to be presented by the directors to the shareholders.[6]

Similarly, in its preamble to Recommendation N18 on Accounting Principles entitled 'Presentation of balance sheet and profit & loss account' the Council of the English Institute remarks

> Whilst it is recognised that the form in which accounts are submitted to shareholders is (subject to compliance with the Companies Act) a matter within the discretion of directors, it is hoped that this Recom-

---

[6] Statement U1, paragraphs 5–6.

mendation will be helpful to members in advising, in appropriate cases, as to what is regarded as the best practice.⁷

The last quotation makes it clear that the professional Institute not only accepts that the responsibility for the choice of accounting principles and procedures rests with the directors, it also adverts to the fact that the only formal external constraint operating upon the directors in making their choice is that imposed by the Companies Act. Indeed, many British accountants appear to feel that the best way in which accounting principles can be improved is by 'strengthening' the provisions of the Act as they relate to financial accounts. The objections to this position will be discussed later in this book.

It is within this general framework that the corpus of rules and procedures (often described in the professional literature as 'principles') has grown up. As new situations have arisen, management has developed new ways of recording and presenting the facts. Many of the more extravagant suggestions have been weeded out but, as we shall see, the residue offers scope for a wide variety of management choice in selecting the 'principles' to be used in any given situation. The only really effective brake on this proliferation has been the exercise by auditors (enforced by statutory authority) of the consistency principle. It is a crude and ineffective weapon.

It is not difficult to understand why there has been such a proliferation of accounting principles. As the complexity of the business world increases management is continually faced with the need and the opportunity to develop new ways of recording and presenting accounting information. It would be naïve to expect them to develop methods and techniques which do not present the position and progress of their company in what they, the management and the directors, consider to be the most favourable light. This is not to impugn their integrity; directors are capitalists and it is in the nature of a capitalist that he should pursue a policy of 'enlightened self-interest'. The matter was put very well in two articles in the Autumn 1965 issue of *Law and Contemporary Problems*.⁸ The late Charles E. Johnson, writing on 'Management and Accounting Principles' said

---

⁷ Issued October 1958.
⁸ See Eldon S. Hendriksen, 'Toward greater comparability through uniformity of accounting principles', *New York Certified Public Accountant*, Vol. XXXVII., No. 2 (February 1967) pp. 105-115.

Management is subject to certain pressures that make unbiased presentation difficult. These pressures include the fact that the statements reflect managerial success or failure, the desire to reduce taxes through specific accounting procedures, the pressure to influence stock prices to the benefit of current stockholders and holders of stock options, and reactions from labour groups and the government.

Robert Sprouse and D. F. Vagts, writing on 'The Accounting Principles Board and Differences and Inconsistencies in Accounting Practice: An Interim Appraisal' in the same issue commented,

Generally, management would find little inconvenience in a lack of inter-firm comparability. Inconvenience is felt primarily by investors and the general public. Therefore, pressures to establish comparability are not likely to be generated by managements.

Of course the role of the professional bodies in Britain has not been entirely passive. From time to time the English Institute has issued Recommendations on Accounting Principles which are designed to indicate 'best' practice, but these recommendations have seldom led the way. On the contrary they have almost invariably consisted of generalisations or codifications of current practice and have been backed up by little or no formal research. What is more serious, the recommendations lack any broad theoretical foundation of general principles, in the true sense of the word 'principles'. The general overall impression is of a something less than energetic attempt to plaster over the cracks as they appear. There is no general plan for the redesign of the structure. Under such circumstances it is perfectly legitimate to argue that accountancy has no real intellectual foundations and that until it does the practice of accountancy is better compared to the practice of wallpapering or plumbing, rather than to the practice of law or medicine.

Some Specific Problems

In order to put this whole problem into better perspective, let us now consider some specific accounting problems and see what the English Institute has recommended.

Some of the following problems may appear to be highly technical and therefore irrelevant to the interests of a small investor. In fact the investor, whatever the size of his holdings, is faced with the task of deciding what to do with his investments in the shares of any particular company. Should he dispose of the shares, should he hold on to them, should he dispose of part of his investment, or should he increase his investment? If he is a potential investor (i.e. does not yet hold *any* shares in the company) he has to decide whether or not to buy any. What he does will depend to a considerable extent on the information which he receives on the company's financial position and progress in the regular accounts of the company. If he is to interpret this information correctly it is essential that he should know precisely how it has been drawn up and, where necessary, he must be able to evaluate the company's stated accounting policies against other acceptable alternatives which might have been adopted instead. It is facile to argue that small investors are too unsophisticated to be able to make this sort of analysis. No one pretends that the man in the street (whom we should encourage to purchase shares in British companies[9]) can be expected to understand the finer points of accounting theory and practice. No one expects the ordinary man in the street to understand the finer points of the law, or to be familiar with the theory and practice of medicine. When he needs advice on these matters he turns to an expert. Similarly the ordinary man in the street, when he needs advice on investment matters, will presumably turn to his banker or stockbroker, or seek the services of an investment advisor or an investment analyst. These experts, however, are just as much outsiders so far as the company is concerned as the small investor. If they are to be able to give sound and intelligible advice to small investors it is necessary that company accounts should provide them with all the information that they need.

But let us not delay any further. Let us look at some of the measurement problems with which the accountant has to deal.

Goodwill

Goodwill can be defined, for our present purposes, as the difference between the value of an enterprise to its owners at a particular date and the net book value of the enterprise at the same date as shown by the balance sheet. Thus, in this sense, goodwill can be seen to represent the extra information that the owners of an enterprise would like to have when they look at its Balance Sheet.

---

[9] If, that is to say, one wishes to encourage the capitalist system.

To say this is of course to over-simplify a very complex problem, and begs the whole question of what we mean when we talk about value to an owner. It also ignores the fact that the value of an enterprise at any point in time cannot be obtained by grossing up the quoted value of its shares on the Stock Exchange at that date. This is because share prices represent values *at the margin* and do not necessarily bear any relation to the value of large blocks of shares.

Despite its importance, goodwill does not appear very frequently in company balance sheets; and when it does, it seldom represents the amount defined above, except in a very special sense. Goodwill is incorporated in a balance sheet only if it has been paid for in the course of a transaction between its past and present owners. It appears at cost, and under the historical cost principle that is the figure at which it remains, unless it is 'amortised'.

Amortisation of goodwill consists in writing it off in the form of periodic annual charges to income over a fixed and usually arbitrary period of years. An alternative practice, followed by some companies, is to write off the whole of purchased goodwill against retained profits at the time of purchase.

Although the nature of goodwill makes it one of the most important concepts in accountancy there has been very little research done on the subject in this country, and the English Institute has little or nothing to say on the subject in its Recommendations.

Revenue from Long-Term Contracts

A contracting company, having entered into a contract to construct say a building or a ship, is faced with the problem of estimating the profit which it expects to earn on the contract, and deciding how to allocate this profit over the accounting periods within which it will be earned, up to the expected date of completion.

Managements of various companies have from time to time adopted various solutions to this problem, and they now stretch all the way from the very conservative approach of deferring the whole of the profits until the contract is completed, to the other extreme of recognising the full profit once the contract is signed. Most companies adopt the procedure of recognising the profit in instalments over the lifetime of the contract, although the basis on which the total profit is allocated between accounting periods can vary widely.

A knowledge of the basis on which the estimates have been made, and the manner in which profits are being allocated to accounting periods, is obviously of major importance to anyone (such as an investor) trying to make sense of a contractor's accounting statements. Yet, once again, this is a matter on which the English Institute has issued no Recommendation.

Leaseholds

Accounting for leaseholds presents a number of problems both to the lessor and the lessee. For the sake of simplicity we shall ignore the former and deal only with the latter.

If a company wishes to acquire a large fixed asset, say a building, it may do so by purchase or, alternatively, it may enter into a long-term contract for the lease of the building from its present owner (or from some new owner, who becomes a party to a 'leaseback' transaction).

If the company purchases the building it acquires a new asset, represented by the cost of the building, and in many cases it will finance the purchase by creating new long-term debt, for example by way of a mortgage or debenture issue.

If, on the other hand, the company leases the building, quite possibly acquiring the same property rights to use and occupancy of the building over its expected life as it would have obtained by purchase, the company is not required to record any asset, and, in particular it will not (in Britain) be expected to record any new liability. Yet it can be argued that the leasehold transaction results in the company acquiring an asset, and incurring a liability for the discounted present value of the future stream of contracted rental payments.

There are many reasons why a company may choose to lease rather than purchase large assets (taxation being one of them), and it has been suggested by financial analysts that a good argument in favour of leasing is that it 'keeps the liability off the Balance Sheet', thereby enhancing the company's credit rating. In fact, the company may end up with a poorer credit rating as a result of leasing rather than purchasing an asset, since more sophisticated analysts will be inclined to impute a liability and, depending on the rate of discount they use, the imputed liability may be larger than the liability which would have been incurred if the asset had been purchased.

Once again, it is clear that this is an area in which investors would be better informed if the professional bodies had issued guidance in the form of a recommendation on the subject. But this has not been done in Britain.

Discount on Debentures

If a company issues debentures with a coupon rate lower than the market rate at the time of issue, the proceeds of sale of the debentures will be less than the face value of the debentures repayable on maturity. The difference is referred to as the discount. It is not an asset, although it is shown as such on some balance sheets. It is in fact a correction to the liability figure, and it should be amortised on the annuity basis over the life of the debentures, in the form of supplementary charges to income (correcting the interest charge).

Although the method described is the correct actuarial method, many companies write off discount to retained profits immediately on issue, while others leave it on the balance sheet (sometimes showing it as an asset) over the life of the Debentures.

None of these problems, and the related problems which arise on refunding or redemption of Debentures, have been adequately dealt with in recommendations of the English Institute. Once again it seems clear that these are matters on which it would be useful to have guidance, and where guidance could easily be given.

The Distinction between the Profit & Loss Account and the Retained Profits Account

Anyone reading a set of company accounts is naturally very interested in the Statement of Profit & Loss. An analysis of the contents of this Statement (particularly when the accounting basis used in arriving at each of the figures is properly disclosed), along with similar statements from previous years, is an extremely important part of the predictive process which underlies all investment decisions.

Quite apart from the principles used in determining the accounting values which appear in the Profit & Loss Statement, there is the question of the *nature* of the items which should properly appear and those which should properly be excluded. The simplistic approach is to say that the Profit & Loss Account should show all revenues and expenses applicable to the accounting period, and should exclude all items of a capital nature.

However, it is not quite as simple as this. There are many items of revenue or expense which may be recognised in a particular accounting period but which an accountant would describe as 'extraordinary' or 'non-recurring', or which 'relate to prior periods'.

Thus, 'extraordinary' items would include profits or losses from

(a) the sale or abandonment of a plant or a significant segment of the business.
(b) the sale of an investment not acquired for re-sale.
(c) the write-off of goodwill due to unusual events or developments within the period.
(d) the condemnation or expropriation of properties.
(e) the major devaluation of a foreign currency.

Adjustments relating to prior periods would include items affecting, for example, income taxes, depreciation provisions, bad debt expenses, profits or losses on contracts, etc., where the difficulties of estimation made it impossible to account for the items properly in the earlier periods to which they relate. It is clear from what has been said already that many accounting valuations necessarily depend upon estimation and, this being so, when what was once the future becomes the past it is possible to measure and adjust such errors of estimation.

The important question is where should such items be located? Should they appear in the Statement of Profit & Loss as part of the measurement of net profit for the year, or should they be treated elsewhere in the accounts (for example in the 'retained profits' account). The English Institute's opinion on this is contained in their Recommendation N18, and reads as follows:

There are differing opinions as to what should be included in the amount shown as the profit or loss of a year. Some consider that it should take into account, subject to separate disclosure of material items in certain circumstances, all profits or losses arising or ascertained within the year, including those items which are the result of activities of the year and others which are the consequence, ascertained within the year, of transactions of earlier years. Others hold that the amount shown as the profit of the year should be restricted to the results of the operations of the year and that all other items should be excluded from the profit or loss of the year as being adjustments of earlier years and should be so shown in the profit and loss account.

Each of these opinions has arguments in its favour and it cannot be said that either of them is generally accepted to the exclusion of the other. Provided that the account is prepared in conformity with either of these opinions and is the result of the consistent application of recognised accounting principles it can properly be said to be true and fair. If a change is made in the *accounting principles* applied and the effect is material, that fact and its consequences would need to be disclosed. (Emphasis added.)[10]

This is not much help to the investor, particularly since a company appears to have a choice each year of deciding which of the two opinions it will select. It is only if the *accounting principles* are changed that there is apparently any inconsistency! Moreover, the Recommendation gives no guidance on the treatment of 'extraordinary' items and seems to be concerned only with prior-period adjustments. Not surprisingly, British company accounts display an egregious diversity of practice in the computation of net profit; the fact that there is usually 'disclosure' of the items included (or excluded) is no excuse since the layman is entitled to expect that the experts know what they are talking about when they say 'profit'. As it is now, the 'experts' are clearly more than somewhat vague on the subject.

A Plethora of 'Principles'

Enough has probably been said to give some idea of the diversity of the problems involved when one talks about accounting principles. Many more examples could be given, but perhaps the reader is prepared to take for granted the fact that wide choices are available to management in the accounting treatment of virtually every item that appears in a set of company accounts.

At this stage it might be useful to look at two areas of accounting practice where the English Institute *has* issued clear-cut recommendations on how items should be treated. The Institute has issued Recommendations on Accounting Principles covering, among other things, the accounting treatment of stocks, of investments, and of depreciation. Let me quote from an article by Professor R. J. Chambers in which he analyses the Institute's position on these matters. Professor Chambers begins by commenting on valuation of stocks.

---

[10] Paragraphs 39 and 40.

The broad bases permitted are cost, net realizable value and replacement price. There are five 'principal' cost methods: unit cost, first-in first-out, average cost, standard cost and adjusted selling price. The first four of these may be computed differently for partly processed and processed stocks; cost may include only direct charges, or direct charges plus portion of all overheads. There are thus three explicitly stated possibilities. In choosing between cost, net realizable value and replacement price, the total stock may be considered as single items, as categories, or as an aggregate . . .

Given three bases, four cost methods, three methods of finding cost (i.e. of treating overheads) and three methods of choosing the final figure, there are $3 \times 4 \times 3 \times 3 = 108$ explicitly permitted methods. If we were to include the various alternative ways of finding depreciation charges and allocating overheads, the total number of possibilites would run into thousands . . .

The recommendations in respect of fixed assets stipulate that historical cost shall be the basis for stating their amounts. But under some circumstances revaluation of assets is permissible (Recommendation N15–30). There are thus two bases. Four methods of writing off depreciation are mentioned (Recommendation N9). It is recognized that for different types of assets different depreciation methods may be appropriate (Recommendation N9–9). If we suppose that there are three classes of fixed assets in most balance sheets, then any combination of three methods is possible. The number of permissible sets of rules for a three-item statement of fixed assets is thus $2 \times 4 \times 3 = 24$.

The recommendation on the treatment of investments (N20) permits four methods of stating the amount of trade investments, four methods for quoted investments, and three methods for shares in subsidiaries. For any company having all three types of investments the number of possible sets of rules for arriving at their aggregate amount is $4 \times 4 \times 3 = 48$.

We will desist. From the above it will be apparent that the number of possible methods, or sets of rules, for obtaining the aggregate amount of the assets of a company which has commodity stocks, three classes of fixed assets and the above-mentioned three classes of security investments is $108 \times 24 \times 48 = 124,416$! And this is only a conservative estimate, which, by including alternatives implicit in some of the rules such as those for depreciation, could be increased at least ten-fold.

A million sets of mutually exclusive rules, each giving a true and fair view of a company's state of affairs and its profits! This is absurd. Where there are so many possible rules there are in effect no rules, and where there are no rules there can be no correspondence, no general comprehensibility, no languge—a set of signs, maybe, but no language. It is as if there were a million people with different footrules, or a million motorists with different road rules. Reason and order are deposed and chaos is enthroned in their place.[11]

---

[11] R. J. Chambers, 'Financial Information and the Securities Market', *Abacus* Vol. 1., No. 1 (September 1965) (pp. 3–30) at pp. 15–16.

It should be noted that Chambers' calculations do not take into account any of the alternatives which we have discussed earlier in this chapter. Taking these into account, along with all of the other alternatives which are available and have not been mentioned here or taken into account by Chambers, there is no doubt that there are at least a million combinations of mutually exclusive ways of arriving at the figure for the net assets in a balance sheet. It should also be understood that none of these combinations will take cognizance of changing price levels, since they are all based on the historical cost principle. It could therefore be argued that all one million of them are irrelevant to the needs of the investor!

Research by the Scottish Institute

Now the reaction of the average chartered accountant when he is confronted with arguments of this kind is to say that the different rules have been devised to fit different circumstances and that they are all required. The point at issue is, of course, in how many circumstances are there several rules, all different, the use of any one of which would have to be accepted by an auditor because he has no criteria by which he can reject it in favour of one of the alternatives. This is the problem which gives rise to much of the difficulty, and this is the problem which needs to be tackled.

One has obviously to keep a sense of proportion. Clearly, there are many cases where companies adopt a particular method or rule which is the only one appropriate to the circumstances. But it is quite absurd to assert that there are not a great many other cases where alternative rules could equally well have been adopted without fear of any qualification by the auditor. Indeed, for a practising public accountant to argue in this way would be dishonest, for practising public accountants know very well what the situation really is.

Yet there have been so many complacent denials that there is really any problem, that it may be useful to quote some paragraphs from an Accounting Research Study published in January 1968 by the Institute of Chartered Accountants of Scotland, dealing with 'Valuation of Stock and Work in Progress'.

The Scottish study points out that a number of large companies use forms of wording in describing the basis of valuation of their stocks which are not very illuminating, such as the following

The amount included for stocks and work-in-progress has been determined for the balance sheet on bases and by methods of computation which are considered appropriate in the circumstances of the company and its subsidiaries and which have been applied consistently.[12]

The study goes on to say that 'the present state of accounting opinion leaves considerable freedom to boards of directors in calculating the "cost" of their stocks, particularly as there has been singularly little discussion in the accounting press on the criteria that should be adopted in selecting the appropriate method. In particular it is not clear whether the test of appropriateness lies in the financial circumstances of the company concerned or in the nature of its trade'.[13]

The study adds that 'many auditors find that a number of methods of valuing stocks is adopted by their clients and that there is considerable variation even within one industry'. Since the descriptions given to the public, including the investor, are generally unilluminating, 'little is known on this subject outside the accounting profession'.[14] This has created a situation, even *within* the profession, where, 'individual auditors are left to speculate whether the methods adopted by their own clients are unusual or whether they are common in industry and commerce generally. An auditor who thinks that his client may be adopting a thoroughly unusual practice may advise him to that effect, but in the present state of general ignorance as to normal practice the auditor is in some difficulty if he wishes to express his disapproval in a more positive way.'[15]

The Scottish Institute's Research Committee attempted to pierce the veils surrounding these mysteries by sending a detailed questionnaire to 1,781 companies. Although the response was disappointing (and this may be quite significant) with usable sets of replies being received from only 302 companies, the Committee concluded that they had collected some very useful information which it would have been difficult to obtain by any other method. Some of the conclusions of the Committee are important and are quoted below:

---

[12] Loc. cit. paragraph 2. Several companies in the survey were found to have used wording of this character, *viz.* British Insulated Callendar's Cables Ltd., Inchcape & Co. Ltd., Reed Paper Group Ltd., Great Universal Stores Ltd., Tube Investments Ltd.
[13] ibid. paragraph 4.
[14] ibid. paragraph 5.
[15] ibid. paragraph 5.

It is safe to draw two conclusions that are of considerable importance to the accounting profession. Broadly stated these are that—
(a) there are considerable variations in the method of calculating the "cost" of stocks for the purpose of annual balance sheets, and
(b) these variations do not arise from the type of business carried on or from the size of the concern.[16]

Further on the Committee concludes that

As to special circumstances "within a particular trade or industry" it is significant that no company (with one possible exception) was able to explain why it had adopted its selected method of calculating cost. In default of other evidence it may be inferred that the method of valuation adopted often depends on the practices and traditions of the past preserved in many cases by the generally accepted view that there should be consistency in the method of valuation. The desire of a successful and expanding company to mitigate its tax liabilities (or of a less prosperous one to state its assets at their full value) may also influence the method of valuation . . .

If it is true that significant differences in methods of stock valuation are frequently not due to objective differences in the circumstances of the organisation or in the type of business, the accountancy profession is facing a serious problem . . . Unless the reader of the accounts has some knowledge of the method of valuation he will be unable to make a proper comparison between two companies with apparently the same type of business and further may draw the wrong conclusion from the recorded results over a period of time . . .

To date the profession both in this country and in North America has tended to avoid any attempt to insist on—or even to recommend—a uniform method of valuation. In this country the profession is in no position to insist and in a matter of this importance it is unlikely that even a recommendation backed by the Councils of the major accountancy bodies would necessarily be observed.[17]

In an Appendix to the study the Committee gives an illustration of the effect of alternative methods of valuing work-in-progress, in one case including both fixed and variable overheads and in the other case including only variable overheads. As the Committee's example shows, even such an apparently trivial difference can result in very wide variations in reported profits.

Another very important area of accounting, and one on which the English Institute has issued detailed pronouncements, is the area of depreciation accounting. In an article in the February 1969 issue of *The Accountant's Magazine* (the journal of the Institute of

---

[16] ibid. paragraph 44.
[17] ibid. paragraphs 47–49.

Chartered Accountants of Scotland), the Scottish Institute's Assistant Secretary (Research) deals with some research which is currently in progress on this subject. A number of very interesting points are made, and the following are of particular relevance to our current discussion.

To sum up, then, accountants are not consistent in the meaning that they attribute to "depreciation", and the term itself is likely to mean something rather different to the majority of those to whom the annual accounts of a business are addressed. (pp. 74–5)

and

To sum up, a study of published accounts, the text of the great number of writings and the answers to the two surveys carried out as part of this research project all lead to the formation of an opinion that there is no real precision either in the nomenclature or in the calculation of what is almost invariably called "depreciation". (p. 76)

and

surveys carried out as part of the research project seem to indicate a lack of real concern about the way in which depreciation is reported and a tendency to follow precedent. (p. 81)

A Clear Need for Reform

Evidence of this kind (which the English Institute has not been conspicuous for collecting or publicising) ought to be sufficient to give pause to even the most complacent of British accountants. It establishes, clearly and authoritatively, that accounting principles are loose and ineffective, and in many cases lead to measurements which are of little or no value even to experts, let alone to the layman. When one also considers that inflation will have made even the best attempts at measurement irrelevant (since they are all tied down to historical cost) one becomes even more sceptical of the value of contemporary British financial accounts. In January 1968 the English Institute published their Statement on Auditing, U8, in which they recommended forms of auditors' reports appropriate for use by their members in the light of Section 14 of the Companies Act 1967. One cannot help but feel that a more appropriate form of audit report would read as follows:

In our opinion, the accounts give a true and fair view of the state of the company's affairs at December 31, 1969 and of its profits for the year ended on that date, in accordance with one or another of the many alternative accounting methods available to management any of which seem to be appropriate in the circumstances, and the accounts comply with the Companies Acts 1948 and 1967.

It is obviously not satisfactory that investors should be served so badly by the accounting profession. It is a situation which cries out for reform. Before offering suggestions as to what ought to be done, let us look at what has been attempted so far, first in America and then in Britain.

11

Accounting Principles: the American Response

The economic systems of the United Kingdom and the United States have much in common, including a large number of international corporations and about half a dozen international firms of public accountants. One can therefore expect that in the long run there will be close similarity between the type of problems dealt with by accountants on both sides of the Atlantic.

Naturally there will be differences of timing and emphasis and, in many cases, of content. Such differences have a great variety of causes, including differences in social and cultural attitudes, in legal requirements, and in political structure. Indeed, we in Britain often congratulate ourselves on the fact that the political and the social structure of Britain are so little affected by the problems which bedevil American life.

British Accountancy Lacking in Vigour?

This is true of accountancy as it is of many other areas. Yet there is no doubt that our reprieve is only a temporary one, in accountancy, at least, and we should do all we can to take advantage of the 'distant early warning system' which the Americans seem to provide. We might also note that although the Americans have serious problems, they deal with most of them with a characteristic vigour which we might well imitate on this side of the Atlantic.

Superior American vigour in accountancy is clearly evident when one compares the efforts made by accountants on the two sides of the Atlantic to supply investors with prompt information in company annual accounts. American corporations, and American auditors, are much quicker in getting their accounts to the shareholders than are their opposite numbers in Britain. This fact is well illustrated in a study made by Mr. P. A. Bird, entitled 'Waiting for the Accounts', and published in *The Accountant* on 9 January 1965 (pages 34–36). Similar studies have been made by others (*see,* for example, P. S. Manley 'The Time Factor in presenting Company Accounts', *The Accountant,* 10 December, 1966, pages 750–753). It is clear that American accountants and auditors are activated by a much stronger sense of urgency, when it comes to informing shareholders, than are British accountants and auditors. Efficiency is no doubt an additional factor.

The quickness of response by American auditors is also evident in the way they reacted to the McKesson & Robbins scandal. This involved larceny on a grand scale by officers of the company, who used some rather ingenious techniques to outwit the company's auditors, Price Waterhouse & Co. As a result of an investigation of the whole affair by the Securities and Exchange Commission, and by the American Institute of Certified Public Accountants, the American profession made it mandatory for American auditors to circularise debtors and attend physical stock-taking of their clients. American auditors who do not perform both these procedures are required to qualify the 'scope' paragraph of their audit report, even if they have satisfied themselves by the use of other procedures. Some people find it rather surprising that the profession in Britain has moved so slowly in this area, even with the hindsight benefit of the American experience; attendance at physical stock-taking, and verification of debtors' balances by direct communication with the debtors, are not yet regarded as mandatory procedures in the United Kingdom. Even the desirability of performing such procedures was not emphasised by the English Institute until it issued statements on the subject in July 1968 and June 1967 respectively.[1]

It is widely believed in this country that the average British business man is possessed of greater integrity than his American counterpart, and such feelings may well justify a less rigorous approach by British auditors. But it is more difficult to account for the tardiness of British auditors and their clients in dealing with annual accounts. It is surely just as important in the United Kingdom as it is in the United States for investors to receive copies of their company's annual accounts as quickly as possible after the financial year end.

---

[1] In Statements U9 and U7.

It is frequently claimed, by apologists for the English Institute, that the accountancy profession in the U.K. is 'the foremost in the world'. Vague statements of this kind, with their natural appeal to the vanity and patriotism of the audience, may have some political value within the English Institute, but one does not establish that one is a leader simply by asserting that it is so. It is not sufficient to be able to 'call spirits from the vasty deep'. They must answer when you call!

The standard piece of evidence of British leadership, offered by the English Institute president in speeches around the country in the Autumn of 1969 (and in his article in *The Times*—see Appendix I), is the fact that the 1967 Companies Act makes Britain 'the only country which requires companies to disclose sales and profits divided by different classes of business'. The fact is that the American Institute, and the SEC, are well aware of the need for such disclosure and intend to require it; their hesitation is because they recognise the importance of first defining how the extremely complex allocation problems should be solved so as to maintain comparability of disclosure between companies. It is noteworthy that the British requirements (which are only just about to come into effect) were imposed by law, not by the profession, and the English Institute has made no attempt so far to deal, by way of a Recommendation, with the tricky theoretical and practical problems which are bound to arise.

Moreover, American companies are, in many cases, already giving this information *voluntarily*. A survey made by the Financial Executives Institute of the 1967 annual reports of 457 American companies showed that 48 per cent 'provided breakdowns of gross revenues by two or more categories' and 9 per cent 'provided a breakdown of earnings to show specific contributions to net income made by product groups or operating units'.[2]

It ill behoves British accountants to claim superiority in matters of disclosure. American standards of disclosure are far higher than those in Britain. American companies have been disclosing turnover figures for many years; it was only in 1967 that this became a British requirement!

---

[2] George Hobgood, 'Voluntary disclosure in 1967 Annual Reports', *Financial Executive,* June 1968 p. 10, and p. 13.

First American Steps towards Reform: the SEC

Professional men on both sides of the Atlantic are of course primarily concerned with the day-to-day operations of their practice. Dramatic events are usually required before major innovations or improvements are introduced. Thus it took the McKesson & Robbins fraud to prod the American profession into tightening up its auditing procedures. An even more dramatic event, which preceded the McKesson & Robbins' case, precipitated action in America to improve accounting principles. This was the Stock Market crash in 1929.

The 1929 crash was preceded by a speculative boom in the virtually unregulated securities market, and although many people were making fortunes during this boom there were others, more thoughtful perhaps, who were very concerned indeed about the quality of the information upon which most of the speculations were based.

In those days the accounting profession in the United Kingdom led the way, and independent audits, which were a common feature of the British scene, were by no means the rule in the United States.

Important critics, including Professor Ripley of Harvard University, began to be heard in the mid-1920s, and the New York Stock Exchange expressed its concern about the need for fuller disclosure in company accounting and reporting. George O. May, a British chartered accountant and the senior partner of Price Waterhouse in the United States, seized the opportunity to develop links with the New York Stock Exchange and he became Chairman of a Committee of the American Institute which was formed to cooperate with the Stock Exchanges.

When the crash came it led to immediate and mounting cries for reform. Ultimately the most important reform, so far as the improvement of accounting principles was concerned, came with the enactment of the Securities Act of 1933 and the Securities Exchange Act in 1934. The first of these gave the Federal Trade Commission authority to administer the new securities legislation; this authority was transferred in 1934 to the newly formed Securities and Exchange Commission (the SEC). As a result of recent amendments, the SEC's authority now extends over the accounting practices of most companies with 500 or more shareholders and over 1 million dollars of total assets whose securities are issued to or traded in by the public.

The legislation gives the Commission extensive powers to prescribe accounting rules. Thus, section 19 of the Securities Acts reads as follows:

The Commission shall have authority from time to time to make, amend, and rescind such rules and regulations as may be necessary to carry out the provisions of this title, including rules and regulations governing registration statements and prospectuses for various classes of securities and issuers, and defining accounting, technical and trade terms used in this title. Among other things, the Commission shall have authority, for the purposes of this title, to prescribe the form or forms in which required information shall be set forth, the items or details to be shown in the balance sheet and earning statement, and the methods to be followed in the preparation of accounts, in the appraisal or valuation of assets and liabilities, in the determination of depreciation and depletion, in the differentiation of recurring and non-recurring income, in the differentiation of investment and operating income, and in the preparation, where the Commission deems it necessary or desirable, of consolidated balance sheets or income accounts of any person directly or indirectly controlling or controlled by the issuer, or any person under direct or indirect common control with the issuer; . . .

The SEC quickly enacted regulation S–X which governs the form and content of the financial statements required to be filed annually with the SEC by all companies under its jurisdiction. However, this regulation was mainly concerned with matters of disclosure and did not attempt to prescribe accounting principles and practices. Nor have the Commission's Accounting Series Releases (of which well over a hundred have now been issued) done much to lay down specific accounting procedures or practices. The general philosophy of the SEC has been to co-operate as closely as possible with the American Institute and to leave to the Institute the primary responsibility for developing and promulgating accounting principles and practices.

It should be emphasised, however, that the fact that all important American companies are required to file annual statements with the SEC, and even more important, the fact that the SEC has the power (if it ever wishes to use it) to step in and prescribe accounting principles and procedures, has provided a very strong stimulus to the improvement of accounting in the United States. Few, if any, American accountants would deny that it is the SEC lurking in the background which has given the American Institute its sense of urgency in promoting the development of good accounting in

America. Until the SEC came along, the American Institute had adopted a relatively passive approach to reform.

Thus, although, as we have seen, the pressure for reform of accounting practices in the U.S. began in the mid-1920s the American profession was still not ready to deal with the SEC legislation when it was enacted over eight years later. Mr. John L. Carey, who retired in 1969 as Administrative Vice-President of the American Institute, has written

> When Bills were introduced in both Houses of Congress—only a few months before final enactment of the Securities Act of 1933 on May 27th of that year—they came as something of a surprise to the profession. No policy positions, no strategy for dealing with such legislation, no constructive proposals for inclusion in such legislation had been worked out. Consequently, instead of having a hand in the drafting of the Securities Act, the profession had to react to drafts prepared by others.[3]

Formation of Committee on Accounting Procedure

However, Mr. May's Committee *had* been at work, and in 1934 they published three recommendations designed to improve financial reporting standards, in part by harnessing the pressure of public opinion. Mr. May's Committee recommended:

> (1) All companies listed on the Stock Exchange should prepare a statement of the methods of accounting and reporting used in their annual accounts. To make it binding on the company the statement was to be adopted by the board of directors, filed with the Stock Exchange, and made available to any shareholder on request.
> (2) Any changes made in these methods were to be notified to the Stock Exchange and to shareholders. Apart from such changes companies were required to assure the Stock Exchange that the methods listed in their statements would be followed consistently.
> (3) Audit reports were to be changed so as to state whether the methods adopted were used, whether they were being applied consistently, and whether they were in conformity with 'accepted principles of accounting'.

Unfortunately, the American Institute never really followed up on these proposals, and it was many years before a serious attempt was made to define the accepted principles of accounting. Consistency became enshrined as a virtue, but the proliferation of accepted

---

[3] John L. Carey, 'The origins of modern financial reporting', *The Journal of Accountancy*, September 1969, p. 43.

methods (unencumbered by any restricting body of principles) combined with consistency to turn a virtue into a vice. Nothing was done to require companies to specify in detail the methods of accounting which they used, and even in the mid-1950s, at the end of his long life, George O. May still regretted that this had never been done.

In 1938, fearing that if it did not move to define accounting principles the SEC would do the job for it, the American Institute set up its Committee on Accounting Procedure. This Committee produced a series of 'Accounting Research Bulletins', 51 of which were issued in the twenty years from 1939 to 1959. Although many of them have been superseded or abandoned as conditions have changed, a number are still in force today.

The Committee on Accounting Procedure adopted an *ad hoc* approach towards its work, and concentrated on putting out fires instead of attempting to fire-proof the building. It dealt with accounting problems on a piecemeal basis as they arose, and it made no attempt to discover or to define a broad encompassing structure of fundamental theory. The Committee's view seemed to be that accounting principles are determined by what accountants do. Since management was given a relatively free hand in deciding what principles they would use (and in developing new principles to meet new circumstances), and since the practitioners sitting on the Committee on Accounting Procedure were naturally somewhat reluctant to condemn methods being used by their own clients, the Committee was not able to exercise much control.

The value of the Research Bulletins was further reduced by the fact that very little research was undertaken in their preparation. Generally speaking, the Bulletins simply enunciated the combined experience of the twenty-one members of the Committee and little if any reasoning was ever offered to support the conclusions spelt out in the Bulletins. No conceptual framework was established, nor was the construction of such a framework attempted; the Committee followed the approach which has been described by George O. May as the 'distillation of experience'. This method of description and codification is a useful preliminary in the development of a body of knowledge but since it consists merely of the exploration of known country, along with the rationalisation of the *status quo,* it is of little help in dealing with new problems. Only by intensive research, and the resultant construction of a conceptual framework, will it be possible to develop a structure of accounting theory and principles which will be anything more than a rehash of what has been done in the past.

This fact became more and more apparent to leading members of the American profession, and in October 1957 the president of the American Institute, Mr. Alvin R. Jennings, announced that he intended to devote his presidential year of office to developing the foundations of an effective research programme. This speech caught the imagination of the American profession and a Committee was formed to develop a research programme. The Committee reported within a year, and in September 1959 the Committee on Accounting Procedure was wound up and replaced by the Accounting Principles Board, whose work was to be supported by a new Accounting Research Divison of the Institute.

The Accounting Principles Board

A conspicuous feature of American accounting for many years has been the important role played by intellectuals and academics in the development of the profession. Academic accountancy is so well established in the United States that practically every important university, and most of the minor universities, have departments of accounting headed by full professors. Most of the important academic literature has been produced in America,[4] and indeed (in contrast to Britain) American practitioners have also made a notable contribution to the intellectual development of the subject. Practitioners such as George O. May, Leonard Spacek, Howard Ross, Paul Grady, Robert Trueblood, William Werntz, and a number of others have played a very important part in developing the intellectual foundations of accounting and in linking together the 'ivory tower' and the 'market place'.

The harnessing of intellectuals in the American Institute's research activities has been particularly noticeable since the formation of the Accounting Research Division of the Institute in 1959. A professor from Berkeley headed up the Research Division for its first three years (Professor Moonitz), and when he returned to Berkeley he was replaced (after a brief interregnum) by another academic, Dr.

---

[4] The rest is largely Australasian, not British.

Storey. Of the ten Accounting Research Studies (each of book length) which have been published so far, one was written by a practitioner, one was written by a retired practitioner, one was prepared by the staff of the Research Division, and all the rest were written by academics in the universities. The purpose of these Research Studies is to 'provide professional accountants and others interested in the development of accounting with an informative discussion of accounting problems under review. The Studies also furnish a vehicle for the exposure of matters for consideration and experimentation prior to the issuance of pronouncements by the Accounting Principles Board'.

Opinions of the Accounting Principles Board, of which 15 have so far been issued,[5] are additional to and will ultimately replace the Accounting Research Bulletins issued by the previous Committee on Accounting Procedure. The APB Opinions are intended to be broader and more comprehensive in their scope than the Bulletins, and it is hoped that they will eventually define a well integrated structure of applied accounting theory. Since the Opinions are supported by research work undertaken by the Accounting Research Division, and since the reasoning behind the opinions is therefore available along with alternatives considered and rejected, it is hoped and expected that the body of Opinions will carry more authority than the Bulletins did.

Indeed, the Council of the American Institute has underlined the authority of the Accounting Principles Board, and its Opinions, by emphasising that the burden of justifying departures from Board Opinions must be assumed by those who adopt other practices. In October 1964 the Council of the Institute provided that

(a) 'Generally accepted accounting principles' are those principles which have substantial authoritative support
(b) Opinions of the Accounting Principles Board constitute 'substantial authoritative support'
(c) 'Substantial authoritative support' can exist for accounting principles that differ from Opinions of the Accounting Principles Board

The action of the American Institute's Council also requires that departures from Board Opinions (and their effect in monetary terms) must be disclosed in footnotes to the annual accounts, or in the

---

[5] As at 31 December 1969.

Auditor's report, when the effect of the departure on the financial statements is material, even though the alternative which has been followed has 'substantial authoritative support'.

In fact, although the new Research Programme is both powerful and promising, it has not been without its disappointments and setbacks. Of the 15 Opinions which have been issued, two (Opinions Nos. 12 and 15) have contained some minor retractions of material previously published, whilst Opinion No. 4 constituted a major retraction of material previously issued in Opinion No. 2. Opinions Nos. 2 and 4 dealt with the accounting for the 'investment credit' (the English and Scottish Institutes have been unable to reconcile their views on a similar problem). The members of the Board were split in their vote on Opinion No. 2, and matters were made worse shortly afterwards when the SEC, in Accounting Series Release No. 96, made it clear that it would not support the Board's Opinion. This effectively forced the Board into its reversal in Opinion No. 4. The chief lesson that can be learnt from this is the importance of research to support the Board's Opinions. For various reasons the Accounting Research Division had undertaken little or no research on the subject of accounting for the investment credit before Opinion No. 2 was issued. Professor Moonitz, who was then the Director of Accounting Research, has since made it clear that this was an important factor in the confusion that followed.[6]

Some critics have discerned a tendency on the part of the APB to drift back into the *ad hoc,* codification, approach of the predecessor Committee on Accounting Procedure. Thus Robert Trueblood, a past president of the American Institute, and senior partner of Touche Ross, has said recently:[7]

I submit that the quality of the Opinions has not been all it should. Many of the Opinions have been codifying in nature. In my view, most of them are too detailed and concern themselves unnecessarily with procedural matters. I am told that, henceforth, attempts will be made to hold Opinions to the enunciation of principle, with procedural details to follow in staff papers. This approach I commend, and I strongly hope

---

[6] *See* his article, 'Some reflections on the Investment Credit Experience', *Journal of Accounting Research*, Vol. 4., No. 1 (Spring 1966) pp. 47–61. *See* also Edward Stamp, 'Some further reflections on the Investment Credit', *Journal of Accounting Research*, Vol. 5., No. 1 (Spring 1967) pp. 124–128.
[7] In a speech delivered to the 53rd Annual Meeting of the American Accounting Association at the University of Notre Dame, 27 August 1969.

that the Board and its staff are prompt in putting the new policy into operation.

Later in the same speech he said

The lack of a set of consistent objectives, and the absence of a statement of the basic purposes of financial reporting, are, in my view, a main reason for the present piecemeal approach to the Board's task. Without a clear definition of purpose there is not solid ground for dealing with individual problems. To formulate acceptable practices on a piecemeal basis without an overall framework of objectives into which they fit is, in my judgment, putting the cart before the horse.

On the other hand, as Mr. Trueblood would undoubtedly be one of the first to agree, the American Institute's new programme, despite the teething troubles which have beset it in its first ten years of life, marks a most important step forward in the life of the accounting profession. The emphasis on fundamental research, the development of close liaison between the academics and the practitioners, and the encouragement of parties outside the profession to participate in the research programme have all contributed in a very important way to the advancement of knowledge. Wide participation in the work of the Accounting Principles Board is encouraged by issuance of 'exposure drafts' of proposed Opinions, thus enabling any interested parties to express their views before the final Opinion is issued. And the requirement that auditors or their clients must disclose material departures from principles laid down by the Board is an important step away from proliferation, and towards the rationalisation, of accounting principles.

There seems little doubt that it is preferable for the development of accounting principles to be undertaken by the profession, through the agency of the Accounting Principles Board, rather than by having the SEC lay down the law. Most leading British practitioners are opposed to the formation of a British SEC, armed with the powers of its American equivalent, and claim to be strongly opposed to regulation by Government authority. Yet the same British accountants will argue that the way to improve company accounting in the United Kingdom is to strengthen the requirements of the Companies Act. They seem to see nothing inconsistent in these two views, and fail to realise that defining good accounting practice by legislation is even more restrictive, bureaucratic, inflexible, and coercive than doing it through the medium of a government agency. Although many American accountants would be glad to see the powers of the SEC curbed, if they were presented with a choice between regulation by the SEC and regulation by Act of Congress there is no doubt that they would choose the former as by far the lesser evil.

If modern accounting practice is to retain flexibility and adaptability, in order to establish and ensure its continuing relevance to the needs of investors, it seems essential that the development of accounting principles should be left in the hands of the profession. Only in this way will the necessary flexibility be preserved. It is curious that those who reject the idea of a British SEC, and who claim to be in favour of maximum flexibility, are at the same time supporting proposals to extend the scope of the Companies Act, a move that will guarantee rigidity rather than flexibility.

12

Accounting Principles: the British Response

Gresham's law of money states that bad money drives out good; it will be clear from what has been said in Chapter 10 that there is also a Gresham's law of accounting principles. Bad accounting principles drive out the good. The situation is aggravated by the fact that it is the directors who choose the accounting principles to be used (the auditor merely exercising a veto); and by the fact that the English Institute attributes such a low utility to published accounts that it is rather difficult to know just what value they are supposed to have at all.

Indeed, little or nothing has been done in Britain even to define what is meant by the term 'accounting principles', and a reader will look in vain through the English Institute's Recommendations on Accounting Principles for any guidance on the matter. (He would be equally frustrated if he sought information from the Institute's Recommendations on the meaning of such obviously important terms as 'a true and fair view', 'profit', 'asset', etc.)

Much has been written on this subject in the United States, and a useful analysis was performed thirty years ago by Gilman in his book *Accounting Concepts of Profit*.[1] Gilman distinguished between conventions (based on general agreement), rules (derived from some authority), doctrines (held as articles of faith), and principles (being fundamental truths from which rules, etc., can be derived). According to Gilman an accounting principle must meet three criteria

(a) It must not be subject to modification by legal fiat or government ruling.
(b) It must be common to all industries.
(c) It must not be changed by the form of proprietorship.

On this basis Gilman found that there were, in 1939, *no* accounting principles!

---

[1] New York: Ronald Press, 1939.

As a first step, the English Institute should decide what are the purposes and objectives of financial accounts, and what is meant by the 'principles of accounting'. Concepts such as conservatism and consistency (doctrines to Gilman) do not merit description as 'principles'. They are more aptly described as doctrines, or perhaps as conventions whose adoption makes life a little safer for the accountant and the auditor in much the same way as the adoption of a left-hand driving convention (imposed as a *rule*!) makes life safer for the motorist.

Similarly, the 'principles' which have been codified in the Recommendations of the English Institute are more aptly described as methods or rules, in many cases as rules of thumb. Again, they make life easier for the accountant and the auditor by giving him sets of formulae which he can apply to his daily tasks, thereby simplifying his work, in much the same way that a motor mechanic uses a repair manual or a cook uses a recipe book. By varying the ingredients in the recipe a cook can produce different varieties of cake and, in the same way, by varying the rules which he uses the accountant can produce different kinds of accounts. Provided he stays within a fairly flexible set of rules his accounts, like the cook's cakes, will be acceptable.

Nevertheless, rules and conventions, however useful, are not principles. They may characterise the early stages of development of a subject (chemistry, for example, in the days of phlogiston, and medicine in the days of the leeches and the sawbones) but as maturity is reached the rules and conventions are supplanted by more basic concepts, 'principles' or 'theories', from which they are derived by a process of deductive logic.

A Suggestion to the English Institute

Accountancy has surely reached the stage where an attempt can be made to formulate principles. Indeed, the need to consider fundamentals is apparent in the consideration of any 'practical' problem, provided one is seeking governing principles and not merely rules or conventions. A convenient illustration of this is provided by the problem of accounting for acquisitions through take-overs or mergers. It is a subject which has vexed American accountants for a number of years, so when Mr. R. G. Leach, president of the English

ACCOUNTING PRINCIPLES: THE BRITISH RESPONSE

Institute, asked me whether I thought different accounting principles should be applied to take-overs and mergers, it was clearly unlikely that, at the stroke of a pen, I would solve a problem which has baffled the Americans for so long. But some suggestions were possible,* thus:

You ask my views on the problem of merger accounting. It is a subject to which I have not given much thought recently, and an area in which I have done no academic research. However, with that caveat, I am glad to give you my views for what they are worth.

Your enquiry relates to the question of the distinctions, if any, which may be drawn between 'mergers' and 'take-overs'. I think it is possible to draw a distinction, but I am not sure that this justifies differences in accounting treatment.

One possible criterion for distinguishing between a merger and a takeover is that the former may be said to have the characteristics of a marriage, whereas the latter can be considered to have some of the features of a rape. But this approach is not very helpful, if for no other reason than the fact that it is difficult to quantify the various factors involved!

A more important criterion is the relative size of the parties involved. A merger can be thought of as arising when the parties (two or more) are of approximately equal size. This immediately raises the question of what one means by 'size'. Should it be based on gross assets, sales, shareholders' equity, or should some other yardstick be used? There is the further problem of defining the limits of approximate equality. How many hairs make a moustache?

A 'take-over' would then presumably be exemplified by situations where the companies fell outside the limits of approximate equality and where the company taken over is manifestly smaller than the other company. There have of course been some cases where the smaller company was the aggressor, but such instances could presumably be embraced by a suitably worded definition!

However, all of this is really semantics. The important question to the accountant is whether such distinctions, if it is possible to draw them, justify two fundamentally different accounting treatments. In particular, is there any justification for carrying forward, in the new 'entity', the assets contributed by the various parties at the book values obtaining before the amalgamation took place? This would be akin to what George May called 'aboriginal' cost accounting. Yet it may be difficult to determine the 'cost' of the assets to the new entity, particularly if the amalgamation transactions were consumated by exchange of shares.

One also has to consider how any 'goodwill' should be treated.

* Extracts from my letter of 10 November 1969 to Mr. Leach, replying to a letter from him dated 5 November 1969.

Should it be carried forward in the new entity (and if so, should it be amortised and, if so, over what period) or should it be written off to retained profits as some accountants have argued? And how does one treat 'retained profits' in the new entity (and what does one *mean* by retained profits in these circumstances).

I think you can probably see the direction in which I am headed. In order to give satisfactory answers to the questions I have posed it is first of all necessary to know the answers to some more fundamental questions. What is the purpose of accounting, and to whom are accounting reports addressed? What is the nature of an accounting entity? On what basis should tangible assets be valued, and must the valuations arise out of 'transactions' in which the 'accounting entity' has been involved? What is the nature of an accounting transaction, and does an exchange of shares in a merger qualify? To what extent does objectivity override relevance in making accounting valuations? What is the nature of 'goodwill' and how should it be measured and handled in accounting reports? What are 'profits' and 'retained profits' and how should they be measured?

These are just a few of the important questions that have to be dealt with, and it is this sort of thing that I have in mind when I talk about the importance of academic research, and of a more fundamental approach towards the solution of accounting problems. I have spent quite a large slice of my life in practice, in a large firm, and I have been well trained in the art of answering questions, like the one you posed, through the exercise of judgment. And, believe me, I have nothing against either judgment or experience. But the trouble with both qualities is that they are subjective, they are not readily transferable, and different people with apparently equal degrees of judgment and experience often come to quite different answers. What we have to do is to analyse the constituents of good accounting judgment and try to determine which of them can be derived by any reasonably intelligent accountant by deduction from established principles and concepts. When we have done this I think it will be much easier to deal with the sort of question you have raised. And there will still be plenty of room for men with good judgment; I see little danger of accountants ending up as glorified form-fillers!

As this letter illustrates, it is only by asking fundamental questions that we can hope to discover fundamental principles. The progress of the medical profession has been based upon the same questioning of fundamentals, and indeed the development of almost any organised branch of knowledge has followed the same path. Nor is the process merely a pattern of deductive enquiry. In the physical sciences, for example, (among the most rigorous of disciplines) the development of principles or theories proceeds by considering apparently unrelated or unexplained facts, by inductive imaginative 'leaps' in which hypotheses are formulated in order to explain the facts, and by the testing of hypotheses through using them to deduce new facts or relationships whose existence (or otherwise) can then be tested by experiment or observation. Hypotheses which successfully survive a series of such tests eventually become elevated to the status of theories. And let us not forget that even scientific theories or laws can eventually be supplanted. For example Newton's laws of gravitation, themselves the product of an imaginative leap, and the source of an enormous volume of deductive scientific reasoning, were eventually supplanted by Einstein's theories of relativity. Nor should we assume that the physical sciences set us an unattainable goal of unambiguous precision and certainty in their theories. Heisenberg's Uncertainty Principle elevates uncertainty to the status of a principle of physical science, and many readers will be aware that the nature of light was explained by two conflicting and concurrent principles, the Wave Theory and the Corpuscular Theory.

Many other examples could be given to illustrate what the term 'principle' means in other areas of knowledge. Many other examples could be given to show that accountancy, merely because it deals with an uncertain and changing world, is not thereby incapable of formulating principles. If uncertainty, complexity, and ambiguity can exist within the structure of scientific theory it would seem craven of accountants to abandon their search for fundamental principles, almost before it has begun, on the grounds that the job is too difficult for them to tackle.

British Academic Accounting

Little has yet been done in Britain to produce a coherent, logical and self-consistent structure of accounting theory. Part of the reason for this can perhaps be understood if we look at the progress of medical research. Few people expect general practitioners to make fundamental contributions to the theory of medicine, or to discover new principles. Fundamental work of this kind is done in research laboratories, mainly in the universities. In British accountancy however, what little research has been undertaken has largely been done on a part-time basis by professional practitioners; *faute de mieux,* since accountancy has scarcely penetrated into the British universities. The reasons for this are complex, and include the curious Oxbridge snobbery of the universities towards anything that smacks of 'vocationalism' (a ludicrous attitude when one considers that law, medicine, and religion are all vocations), and partly because of the generally anti-intellectual attitude of the British practitioners towards the development of the foundations of their subject.

An illustration of the relatively slow rate of academic development in accountancy in Britain can be obtained by comparison with what has occurred in Australia, a much smaller country. The first full-time Chair of Accounting in Australia was created in 1955 with the appointment of Sir Alexander Fitzgerald to the Chair in Melbourne. In the fourteen years since then eleven more full-time Chairs have been created at various universities in Australia, and the resultant output of academic writing and research in Australia has been ample and impressive. The first full-time Chair of accounting in Britain was created much earlier than in Australia, in 1948, with the appointment of William Baxter (a former lecturer at Edinburgh University and Professor at Cape Town) to the Chair at the London School of Economics. In the subsequent twenty-one years, only eight more full-time Chairs have been created. Indeed, in that period of time a Chair of Accountancy has been liquidated; when the English Institute took over the Society of Incorporated Accountants and Auditors it liquidated the Society's Stamp-Martin Chair of Accountancy, along with *Accounting Research*, a journal which had enjoyed a high reputation throughout the world for the quality of its articles.[2]

There is no room for complacency on the subject. In the article 'The trouble with accountants' (*Financial Times*, 10 November 1969), referred to earlier, it was stated that accountancy in Britain 'is not exactly an unlettered profession, since there are now nine Chairs of Accountancy in the U.K.' This is nothing to write home, or to Australia, about. There are eight full professors of Law, and twenty-three full professors of Medicine, in Edinburgh University alone!

British Progress to Date

What has in fact been done to date in Britain to deal with the

---

[2] It was announced in the December 1969 issue of *Accountancy* that it is intended to revive *Accounting Research*. However it will be edited by the present editorial staff of *Accountancy*. (*See* Appendix II)

accounting principles dilemma? As we have seen, very little has been done in the way of fundamental thinking or research. The main emphasis has been a preoccupation with rules, procedures, and technique. The English Institute has published, and continues to publish, Recommendations on Accounting Principles and Recommendations on Auditing but, unlike the American Institute, it has made no attempt to engage in serious fundamental research.

Surprisingly, when one considers the quality of intellectual life in Scotland, the Scottish Institute has so far failed to give a lead in this matter, although, as we have seen in Chapter 10, the Scottish Institute commissions and publishes Research Studies from time to time, and some of these have been very helpful in concentrating attention on important problems.

The English Institute, as its president Mr. Leach stated in replying to my article in *The Times* (*see* Appendix I), 'has responded by formulating broad principles which are capable of being applied differently in different circumstances'. Later, in the same article, he says 'the real difficulty is not the absence or multitude of accounting principles but applying them to the facts of a particular business'. Unfortunately, as the Scottish Research Study on stock valuation has shown, too many of these broad principles are capable of being applied differently in the *same* circumstances.

Further on in his article, Mr. Leach, in discussing problems of valuation, mentions that 'at the start of the take-over movement after the War, we saw instances of undervaluation of assets and of consequent damage to shareholders'. Yet, as we have already seen, the English Institute persists in recommending the historical cost principle to its members, despite the fact that this has obviously resulted in balance sheets which undervalue the assets and cause very serious distortions in the measurement of income!

Not only are the English Institute's so-called 'principles' capable of being applied differently to the same circumstances, the professional bodies in England and Scotland have proved themselves capable of developing different principles to suit the same sets of facts. Thus, in the winter of 1966/7 the two Institutes produced two entirely different principles governing the treatment of investment grants. (The English Institute's proposals were contained in a Recommendation, whilst the Scottish Institute's were contained in a paper published by their Research and Publications Committee.)

The English Institute proposed two alternative, but essentially similar, methods by which the tax-paid benefit from the grant would be brought into income over the life of the assets to which the grant relates. The Scottish Institute rejected this procedure, recommending that the tax-paid benefit should be treated as a capital item and credited to a capital reserve. No part of it would thus enter into the computation of profits. (As we saw in Chapter 11 similar inconsistencies have arisen in the United States, but there the conflict was between the American Institute of Certified Public Accountants and the Securities and Exchange Commission.)[3] So far there has been no reconciliation between the English and Scottish Institutes on this matter, although it is understood that Israeli accountants are now adopting the Scottish system!

As William Werntz, a former Chief Accountant of the Securities and Exchange Commission, and later a partner in the major public accounting firm of Touche Ross, stated in discussing the problem

In some areas agreement on basic postulates ought to enable us to resolve existing basic disagreements. As good an example as any would be the controversy over income tax allocation. Surely the important divergence in results which comes about by the use or non-use of income tax allocation must flow from differing basic assumptions—not from differences in facts or differences in methods of making estimates. The same is probably true of some of the other critical problems facing us today, such as whether to recognise price level adjustments, to capitalise leases, or to write off or capitalise intangible drilling costs, gross or net of taxes.[4]

As Werntz makes clear, judgements will always be required in accountancy in distinguishing between different situations, and in making the estimates of the future which are required in applying many asset valuation procedures. But if we are to narrow the areas of difference it is surely clear that accountants must develop a fundamental theory which will specify the basic assumptions from which everything else begins.

The first step, if any progress is to be made, is to abandon the sense of apathy and complacency which seems to overwhelm the

---

[3] Who were not so far apart as the English and the Scots, since the AICPA and the SEC both accepted that the benefit should flow into income. They differed on the question of the timing.

[4] William W. Werntz, 'What are the basic accounting postulates', *The Quarterly* (Touche Ross & Co.) Vol. 8., No. 1 (March 1962) pp. 2-11.

British accountant whenever such matters are seriously discussed. The complacency is evident in Mr. Leach's reply (*see* Appendix I) to my article in *The Times*.[5] This chapter will end with a brief illustration of the apathy.

The Apathy of British Accountants

In its issue dated 28 June 1969, the weekly journal *The Accountant* published a summary of the 1968 accounts of Cunard which showed that nearly £10 million had been written off the cost of the Queen Elizabeth 2 before the ship had even made her maiden voyage to New York. This was done, according to Sir Basil Smallpiece (a member of the English Institute, and Chairman of Cunard) in order to reduce the book value of the ship to its 'economic value'. This, he said, would establish the company on a firm financial basis for the future with no deadwood.

British accounting eccentricities seldom make news in the American professional literature, but this particular item was reported in the August 1969 issue of the *Journal of Accountancy* (the journal of the American Institute).

The 12 July 1969 issue of *The Accountant* published a letter from Mr. W. Robinson, F.C.A., who said that he was disappointed that there had been no criticism of Cunard's accounts in the 28 June issue. He remarked that *The Financial Times* comments on the 'accounting manipulations' of Cunard might be thought to have been 'too kind'. Mr. Robinson said that exceptional items charged to reserves amount to no less than £17½ million 'and the plain fact is that in 1968 and in future years the profit & loss accounts will be undercharged by that amount at least. It is therefore not the "deadwood" of the past which is being cut out but the possible future losses which are being quietly "buried in advance".' Mr Robinson ended his letter by hoping that there would be a general

---

[5] Although there is undoubtedly a distinct note of complacency in Mr. Leach's reply, it is fair to reflect that he wrote it at a time when many members of the English Institute—rightly or wrongly, it makes no matter—were highly indignant at my criticisms. They were not used to being criticised by academics. It was therefore necessary for the president to emphasise the important contributions which the Institute has undoubtedly made. Moreover, Mr. Leach subsequently demonstrated his leadership with the 'Statement of Intent' (see p. 146). Indeed the speed and vigour of the Institute's response in this instance has been remarkable.

expression of views on this matter in *The Accountant*'s correspondence columns.

The 2 August issue of *The Accountant* published a further letter by Mr. Robinson in which he expressed his disappointment that no one had commented on his letter of 12 July. If trained accountants accept what was done without question, he stated, it is hardly surprising that untrained sharcholders show lack of interest.

Despite this further plea, nothing appeared on the subject until the 18 October 1969 issue of *The Accountant* published a letter from Michael Greener, referring to Mr. Robinson's complaint about the lack of response to his (Robinson's) detailed criticisms of the Cunard accounts. Mr. Greener said that he wished to assure Mr. Robinson, 'from personal experience, that it is not always a matter of apathy but rather of disenchantment. One protests, objects, but no one answers and one suspects that no one cares. Perhaps interests are too vested to be vexed'.

Mr. Greener then went on to complain about the treatment of development expenditure in the accounts of the Thomson Organisation Ltd., applicable to *The Times* newspaper. Development expenditure was capitalised instead of being written off against current profits (these are quite acceptable alternatives, to accountants) but, as Mr. Greener pointed out, the capitalisation was effected by charging the expenditures against capital reserve. In this way no part of the development expenditures would ever appear as an amortisation charge against future profits.

Mr. Greener's comments, like those of Mr. Robinson's, have been ignored by readers of *The Accountant*.

It would surely be disingenuous to suggest that British accountants have been taking a lively and active interest in the solution of the unsolved problems of accountancy.

There is much to be done. Before suggesting what it is, let us look for a moment at the role of the auditor.

13

'The True and Fair View'—the Ambiguous Position of the Auditor

As the English Institute states in its preamble to its first Statement on Auditing, 'Auditing is an important professional task carrying heavy responsibility and calling for commensurate skill and judgment'. This statement is undoubtedly true and, as we shall see later, the role of the auditor is so important to the health and strength of the free enterprise system that it could rightly be regarded as one of the keystones in the arches making up that system.

Yet in some ways, by comparison with the legal and medical professions for example, the lot of the auditor appears to be a far from unhappy one. Thus the average lawyer may expect that on average he will lose about half of his cases. Any doctor is well aware of the truth of Keynes' remark that in the long run we are all dead. By comparison, an auditor of average competence can expect to lose relatively few clients, and even in North America where competition between auditors is more fierce than it is in Britain and where the risks of professional piracy are greater, there is relatively little turnover of clients between firms of auditors.

Who is the Auditor's Client?

This is a fairly clear indication of client satisfaction with the work done by the auditor. In the case of public companies (with which we are mainly concerned in this book) the 'client' is ostensibly the body of shareholders. Auditors are appointed, and reappointed, by the shareholders voting in general meeting. Auditors' remuneration is also ostensibly fixed by the shareholders. In practice however it is the management and the directors with whom the auditor deals when he deals with the company. It is only in the most unusual circumstances that an auditor has any direct communication with the average shareholder. Even the auditor's statutory report to the shareholders is circulated by the directors, as an appendage to the annual accounts. So it is clearly extremely important for auditors to maintain close and cordial relations with their client company's directors. And indeed, in some instances there may be some doubt about just who the auditor's client really is—the shareholders or the directors. Thus, the Council of the English Institute, in discussing the problem of unlawful acts or defaults by clients of members makes the following statement:

> In considering the advice given in this statement it is important to bear in mind that in the case of a company governed by the Companies Acts 1948 to 1967 the auditor's client is the company and not the directors. Where, however, the directors have so acted as to result in the company defrauding the Revenue or committing other offences, references in this statement to the 'client' should be regarded in the first instance as referring to the directors of the company; for example, where it is necessary for the member to advise a client to make a full disclosure to the Revenue the advice should be given to the directors.[1]

It is clear that there is a certain degree of ambiguity about the meaning of the term 'client', and it will become apparent later that the role of the auditor contains other more serious ambiguities.

The fact is that the ordinary shareholder of a public company really has no way of knowing whether 'his' auditors are doing their job properly or not. He is dealing with a priesthood, whose arcane rites are beyond his ken; unlike his priest however, he is unlikely ever to see his auditor at work or to have any knowledge of the margin of error within which he operates. As we have seen, the margin of error is in fact quite comfortably wide, set as it is by the generous boundaries of 'generally accepted accounting principles'. It is only when a client company really gets into difficulties that the work of the auditor is likely to be called under review. Even then, anyone who questions the value of the auditor's work runs the risk of being accused of making auditors into 'scapegoats'.

It must however be emphasised that the role of the auditor in a capitalist system *is* an extremely important one. The pace of technological development has been so great in this century that few if any important industries are now dominated by privately owned

---

[1] Statement S12, paragraph 45.

companies. Industry and commerce now require capital in such large amounts that directors of public companies can seldom supply more than a very small fraction of the total capital required. The rest is obtained from outsiders who, although the owners of the enterprise, are largely divorced from its management. If such a system of financing is to operate successfully, and if the securities markets are to function effectively, it becomes necessary for management and directors to supply shareholders with periodic reports containing detailed financial information on how the company has fared since the previous report. These reports, or accounts, along with other information, form the basis on which investors make their decisions. Since the management has full control over the company's accounting system, and since management is entitled to select the accounting principles used in preparing the accounts, it is clear that there is a serious risk that, on occasion, management may feel that it is in its own interests to distort or suppress information which shareholders ought to have.

This is where the auditor comes in. His function is to make an independent examination of the accounts prepared by the management, and to formulate and express his opinion as to whether or not the accounts give 'a true and fair view' of the company's affairs. It is this report which is submitted to the shareholders along with the annual accounts.

The function of the auditor is thus to lend credibility to the financial statements submitted by the directors to the shareholders. Without the auditor's report, the shareholders would be left in doubt about the reliability of the accounts, and this could weaken and possibly even destroy their confidence in the company, and indeed in the whole capitalist system. It is in this sense that the role of the auditor can be likened to that of a keystone in an arch; by helping to establish and maintain investor confidence in the integrity of the securities markets the auditor contributes in a very important way to the strength of the capitalist system. It is thus very much in the public interest that the auditor should be seen to be completely independent of management. Indeed, the social function of the large corporation has now become so important that the auditor ought to be seen to be acting with the *public interest* in mind as well as the interests of the present shareholders of the company. Auditors certainly ought to consider the interests of *prospective* shareholders. (In fact, since shareholdings in public companies change, sometimes rapidly and substantially, as shares are traded on the Stock Exchange, the composition of the body of shareholders may be quite different from one year to the next.)

Some Difficulties for the Auditor

From what has been said in earlier chapters it will be clear that the auditor has some difficulty in determining what is in fact 'a true and fair view'. Even the phrase itself is ambiguous, since presumably if the accounts give a 'true' view they must also give a 'fair' view. That it is apparently possible for a true view of a company's financial situation to be at the same time an unfair view (particularly if 'full disclosure' of all 'material' facts has taken place so that the 'whole truth' is given) gives some further indication of the unsatisfactory state of accounting 'principles'.

The anomalies of the auditor's position are compounded when it is remembered that, as the English Institute has stated, 'responsibility for the accounts and financial control of a company rests upon the directors', and the directors' duties include 'the preparation of annual accounts showing the true and fair view required by the Act' with 'the responsibility for establishing and maintaining an adequate system of internal control'.

As we have explained in earlier chapters, this can be summed up by saying that management chooses the system, the rules, and the procedures, and management prepares the financial accounts. The auditor's job is to decide whether management's choice of rules can be said to present a 'true and fair view', even though the auditor may feel that quite a different selection of rules would also have produced 'a true and fair view' and might even have produced a truer and a fairer view!

If the auditor is not satisfied with what the directors have done he has a powerful sanction available to him. He can qualify his report. But unless his 'client's' accounts are clearly outside the ambit of that large and fuzzy area known as 'generally accepted accounting principles' the auditor will be under a great deal of pressure to accept the directors' views, and he may find it difficult, if not impossible, to insist on a change to a truer or a fairer set of rules. His difficulties are compounded by the fact that auditors have tended to make such a virtue out of consistency that the importance of comparability of accounts between one company and another in the same industry has been virtually ignored. The directors, faced with arguments from an auditor urging a change, will often be able to clinch the discussion in their own favour by pointing out the danger of violating the all-important rule of consistency.

Another difficulty faced by the auditor is the fact that all of the discussions which occur on matters like this take place behind veils of secrecy, and the real client (the shareholders) are not even entitled to know that the arguments occurred, let alone the details, except on those rare occasions when a qualified report is issued. Even when he qualifies, the auditor cannot publish the details of the arguments which took place.

If the client company is in financial difficulties the auditor is faced with a further problem. In such cases directors are often very anxious to adopt methods of presentation which give the best possible impression of the company's position and prospects. The auditor may feel that if he should refuse to go along with the directors, and if he issues a qualified report, the company may crash. He may well feel that the company will crash anyway, but he knows that if he issues a qualified report it will be quite impossible for him, after the crash, to establish that if he had not qualified the crash would still have occurred. Under such circumstances the pressures to do nothing are obvious.

The Auditor as a Judge

It will be clear from what has been said that the role of an auditor is essentially that of a Judge. Even in the conventional view of these matters the auditor is required to formulate his independent judgement on what the directors have done, and to render this judgement to his 'client', the shareholders. Even in the conventional view the auditor acts as a Judge. But the modern public company fills such an important role in the economic structure of the nation, and the effective functioning of the securities markets is so important to the free enterprise system, that the auditor's constituency now embraces the whole public interest. It can no longer be argued that an auditor is merely concerned with the interests of the present shareholders of the company, without regard to the interests and the requirements of the public at large, including potential shareholders, creditors and potential creditors, employees, labour unions, and government.

If the auditor is to act as a Judge, and if he is to act effectively in the public interest, it is necessary that he should enjoy, and be seen to enjoy, complete independence of those whose actions he is called upon to judge, namely the directors of the company. The relationship between a Judge in a court of law and the parties before him, whose actions are being judged, is one which is carefully defined. It is a relationship which is carefully defined so as to protect the public interest and to ensure that the public has complete confidence in the operation of the legal system. It is instructive to consider some of the characteristics of a Judge in a court of law and to see to what extent they are enjoyed by the auditor *qua* Judge.

(1) Legal arguments are almost invariably heard in open court. Only in the most unusual circumstances, espionage cases for example, are proceedings held *in camera*. Open decisions openly arrived at are an integral part of a system where justice is not only done but seen to be done.

As we have already seen, the situation in the case of the audit judgement is quite different. Auditor's judgements are invariably made *in camera*, even though most of the material cannot be considered confidential. There is room for much more disclosure of the evidence upon which audit judgments are made, even if it is necessary to continue to keep matters such as executive's salaries and bonuses *sub rosa*. In fact, recent company legislation has now made it mandatory for companies to disclose items such as the chairman's emoluments, sales turnover, and other items which had hitherto been regarded as strictly confidential. So 'confidentiality' is a poor excuse.

(2) The decisions of the Judge in a court of law are published along with the reasons for the judgement, and they form part of the permanent records of the legal system.

No such procedure is followed in accounting practice, although it would obviously be of great interest and value if such material were made available to shareholders and other investors, other auditors, investment analysts, etc. Under the present system none of these interested parties, all of whom have a legitimate interest in the facts, is entitled to access to this information. Consequently it becomes extremely difficult to assess and analyse the auditor's judgement.

(3) Judgements in a court of law are bound by precedents established in earlier cases, as well as by statute law.

As we have seen, audit judgements are heavily influenced by the doctrine of consistency. But in view of the plethora of alternative 'principles' available to a company's management, the fact that a company's presentation is consistent with its practice in earlier years is by no means any guarantee that it is consistent with the practice being followed by other companies in similar circumstances or in the same industry. The price of consistency in this situation is loss of comparability and a failure to treat like things as if they were alike. Essentially the situation in accountancy is that management is required to act consistently with the rules of the game which it itself has elected to play by. In legal practice the actions of the parties are judged against a framework of rules which are established by the system, not by the parties themselves.

(4) The likelihood that a Judge in a court of law will act in the public interest, and the confidence of the public that he will do so, is increased by the fact that Judges are paid independently by the State. It would be regarded as unthinkable for a Judge to look to the parties appearing before him for his remuneration.

By contrast, the auditor is paid by his client's company, and the usual procedure is that the fee is fixed by negotiation with the directors and then approved by the shareholders. The public interest is not represented in this procedure at all and since, as the quotation on page 120 indicates, there is some ambiguity as to just who exactly is the client (particularly if the 'client' has done wrong) the auditor cannot be said to be independently remunerated, in any sense.

(5) The Judge in a court of law is appointed independently of the parties who appear before him, or who are likely to appear before him. The usual procedure in this country is that the Judge is appointed by the Crown. The fact that such a method of appointment is an important ingredient of public confidence is evident if one thinks of the position in many American state courts. Many of their Judges stand for election in a political campaign and actively canvas the voting support of people who may appear before them in the future. Such a system does not exist in Britain, and it is doubtful that its introduction would increase the confidence of the British people in their judicial system.

As we have seen, auditors are appointed by their clients, the shareholders, in general meeting, and they are usually selected by the directors whom they are required to judge.

(6) The Judge in a court of law enjoys full security of tenure, and he cannot be removed from office by the action of parties who have appeared before him and who are dissatisfied with his decisions. Without such security of tenure the confidence of the public in a Judge's impartiality would be impaired.

The auditor, on the other hand, enjoys no such security of tenure, and although his interests are protected to some extent by the Companies Act, and although he may win the support of the shareholders if he should come into conflict with the directors, he has no *guarantee* that this will be the case whilst he is attempting to make decisions on the propriety of directors' actions. Thus the Judge's independence and impartiality are confirmed by a system which invests him with every aspect of their appearance, as well as their reality. The Judge's integrity therefore becomes *pro non scripto*. With the auditor, however, the formal relationships do not imply independence, and integrity must be invoked to support the contention of independence. Yet integrity is not enhanced if it has to be openly proclaimed in order to support one's position. As in the case of the Judge, it ought to be *pro non scripto*.

(7) Judges in a court of law are not permitted to have any financial or personal interest in the parties who appear before them. If they do have such an interest, they are required, not simply to disclose it, but to debar themselves from the case. The public's confidence in the impartiality of Judges depends heavily upon this, and the resignation of Mr. Fortas from the United States Supreme Court and the failure of the United States Senate to approve the appointment of Mr. Haynsworth to the Supreme Court give clear and convincing evidence of the continuing importance of this principle in the American system as well as in the British system.

By contrast there is nothing to prevent auditors from owning shares in their client companies, and indeed some auditors feel that it is a mark of their confidence in their client that they should have a financial stake in his company. Not only may an auditor own shares in a client company, he is not required to disclose whether or not he does own any shares, how many he owns, or whether he has acquired or disposed of any during the current financial year. Thus the shareholder, reading the auditor's report, has no way of telling to what extent, if any, the auditor is financially interested in the company. Whilst some shareholders may not perhaps feel that this prejudices the auditor's position, the public at large can surely not regard such a situation as providing any guarantee of the impartiality of the auditor.

(8) Judges in a court of law cannot advise the parties who appear before them. It would be absurd to think that the public would accept a situation where Judges were permitted to render legal advice, for a fee, to the people whom they are required to judge.

Yet auditing firms derive very substantial fees from the provision of tax advice, and management advisory services, and various other ancillary services, to their audit clients. Not only does this tend to make the auditor identify himself with the interests of the client company and its management, it also tends to make the auditor identify himself with some of the decisions taken by the management. This makes it all the more difficult for him to seem to render an impartial judgement on the reporting of the results of these decisions in the annual accounts.

For all of these reasons it is possible to argue very strongly that the auditor, under the present system, is not independent of his client, despite the fact that it is in the public interest that he should be independent. It is not sufficient for auditors to reply that their independence is a 'state of mind' and that this is guaranteed by their integrity. The independence of one's state of mind can in the last analysis only be judged by the products of the state of mind; in the case of the auditor this product is his report. The argument is circular and it begs the question. Indeed, in view of the thousands if not millions of alternative combinations of ways of presenting a 'true and fair view', it might be said to beg a million questions. Nor should one be sidetracked by the assertion that the questions raised above, about the auditor's independence, constitute an aspersion upon the auditor's integrity. The system described above, as it applies to Judges in courts of law, has been devised and has evolved not because people question the integrity of their Judges, but because they believe that justice must not only be done but be seen to be done. *The integrity of auditors is not in question in these matters.* Auditors are not under suspicion; the point is they must be *above* suspicion. (At the same time members of the auditing profession should be careful not to attempt to defend themselves against imaginary attacks on their integrity by impugning the integrity of their critics.) Nor does it make much sense to attempt to answer the arguments which have been presented above by asking the critics to produce evidence that accountants are not saints. It is because accountants are known to be human (*pace* Elbert Hubbard) that the appearance as well as the reality of their independence is important.

It must now be obvious that the position of the auditor must be considered very carefully when one is attempting to assess the overall reforms which need to be made in the accounting profession. Auditors are effectively being asked to play the part of Judges in a game where the players make many of the rules, and where the auditor lacks many of the necessary attributes of independence. The profession is involved because it recognises that it has some responsibility for the rule-making function. This responsibility is recognised by the English Institute when it issues its Recommendations on Accounting Principles. Unfortunately, far too many members of the accounting profession feel that the best way to improve the rule-making function is to hand the job over to Parliament by having the Companies Act define in greater detail what is required. If the accountancy profession adopts this as an official policy it will be abdicating its responsibility. Members of Parliament, and their legal draughtsmen, are generally unskilled in accountancy and nothing would be better calculated to destroy the flexibility in the present system than having accounting rules enshrined as Acts of Parliament. As explained in Chapter 15, the best way to add 'teeth' to the auditor's position is to give the accounting profession statutory authority, in the Companies Act, to define accounting principles and good accounting practice. Accounting principles, and rules of disclosure in financial statements, should not be defined in schedules to the Companies Act, they ought to be defined and enforced by the accountancy profession.

Note: The main body of this section of the book is primarily concerned with accounting principles. I have already proposed two alternative solutions to the problem of the auditor's independence and readers who are interested will find them covered in detail in Appendix III.

14

Uniformity or Flexibility: the False Dichotomy

Arguments in favour of reform always meet with some opposition, and when one is arguing for the reform of something as conservative as the attitudes of British accountants opposition is inevitable. A programme for reform will win support from the progressive younger members; it will also appeal to some (but by no means all) of the senior members of the profession. In between is a group who will always feel most comfortable with the *status quo*.

One superficially rational argument in favour of the *status quo* consists in arguing for flexibility as against uniformity. The argument runs somewhat as follows: We live in a complex and changing world and the only sensible way for accountants to deal with such a situation is to recognise the limitations of accounts, and to maintain an open-minded and flexible attitude, tempered by consistency. The goal of 'uniformity' with its connotations of a 'rigid set of rules' imposing a strait-jacket on progress should be avoided at all costs.

The argument has a seductive plausibility (most arguments in favour of the *status quo* do, particularly to dinosaurs). But in fact the dichotomy is a false one and it is the purpose of this chapter to explain why.

The Utility of Financial Accounts

First of all, however, it will be helpful to restate the basic problem. In essence the problem is that the users of published audited financial accounts are being misinformed because they are not being supplied with information relevant to their needs as users. Thus, to quote the English Institute

> The function of a balance sheet is to give a true and fair view of the state of affairs of the company as on a particular date . . . a true and fair view implies the consistent application of generally accepted

[accounting] principles . . . a balance sheet is therefore mainly an historical document which does not purport to show the realisable value of assets such as goodwill, land, buildings, plant and machinery; nor does it normally purport to show the realisable value of assets such as stock-in-trade. Thus a balance sheet is not a statement of the net worth of the undertaking and this is normally so even where there has been a revaluation of assets and the balance sheet amounts are based on the revaluation instead of on cost (N18, paragraphs 3 and 4).

Again,

. . . the results shown by accounts prepared on the basis of historical cost are not a measure of increase or decrease in wealth in terms of purchasing power; nor do the results necessarily represent the amount which can prudently be regarded as available for distribution, having regard to the financial requirements of the business. Similarly the results shown by such accounts are not necessarily suitable for purposes such as price fixing, wage negotiations and taxation, unless in using them for these purposes due regard is paid to the amount of profit which has been retained in the business for its maintenance. (N15, paragraph 28.)

Again,

No claim by an individual shareholder, however, would succeed in respect of loss suffered through his own investment decisions made on the strength of misleading company accounts supported by an auditors' report containing negligent misrepresentations, since the purpose for which annual accounts are normally prepared is not to enable individual shareholders to take investment decisions. (S8, paragraph 8 (b).)

As we have argued earlier, statements of this kind must make the investor wonder what sense can be attached to the phrase 'true and fair view', and what value, if any, there is in a set of audited financial accounts.

Economists must also feel baffled by statements of this kind, and wonder what value *they* can attach to financial accounts, and whether financial accounts serve any useful purpose in the process of making efficient allocation of economic resources.

A Plethora of Methods

All of this arises, as we have seen in earlier chapters, because management usually has a choice of many alternative ways of measuring and reporting financial data, any one of the several different alternatives leading to results which are regarded as 'generally acceptable' by the accountancy profession. Auditors (who may lack the degree of independence requisite to such a delicate situation) are required to judge whether management's selection of 'principles' falls between the wide boundaries encompassing 'the true and fair view'. The fact that the 'true and fair view' (whichever one happens to be selected) may have little or no relevance to the needs of the user of the financial accounts is not regarded as important. Flexibility, so long as it is anchored down by consistency, becomes a virtue in itself even although it leads to accounts which are consistently useless, consistently irrelevant, and consistently non-comparable with accounts of other companies in which an investor is also interested (even those in the same industry).

It can be seen that the root of the problem lies in the wide range of choice open to management in the selection of accounting principles. We have traced the origins of this multiplicity of accounting principles in earlier chapters, where we have also emphasised that the interests of management do not necessarily coincide with the interests of shareholders, to say nothing of other interested parties (such as potential shareholders), and management will naturally select the accounting methods which it believes best serve its own interests. Thus a plethora of alternative ways of presenting the same transaction in published accounts is not likely to encourage standards of financial reporting which will best serve the needs of the users of published financial accounts. On the contrary, in many cases the bad methods will drive out the good. Some accountants have argued that a process of natural evolution, of *laissez faire,* is the one best calculated to achieve improvement in accounting principles. As in economics, such a view assumes 'an invisible hand' which will guide accountancy to Utopia; unfortunately, the invisible hand, in accountancy as in economics, is not only invisible but non-existent.

A wide range of choice is even regarded, by some, as a good thing in itself. Multiplicity becomes equated with freedom; an editorial in the November 1969 issue of *Accountancy* (the journal of the English Institute) argues that 'it is a typical British compromise that there is frequently a choice of acceptable methods of dealing with a particular type of transaction, a choice open to the management of the individual business in preparing its accounts'.[1] One can be forgiven for making a virtue out of necessity, but it scarcely seems necessary to make a virtue out of a fallacy.

Management's Attitudes to the Future

Another more subtle argument, which has been used to justify the remarkable discrepancies which often come to light after a take-over, is that the range of choice available to management is justified because of the corresponding range of management policies and attitudes towards the future. There is sense in this line of argument, since many valuations depend upon expectations and intentions. If management changes, then perhaps a change in the bases of valuation of assets can be justified on the grounds that the new management has an entirely different set of intentions and expectations from the management which it has supplanted.

A serious drawback to this argument is the difficulty of making any kind of objective measurement of 'expectations and intentions', especially those of a large and changing body of men. (As we have seen, auditors have a passion for objectivity which is one reason why they are so attached to the historical cost convention, and it is surprising that leading auditors advance this particular argument in justification of flexibility.) When a new management takes over an existing firm they will clearly have a very strong incentive to write off as much as they can in the first year after the take-over. If necessary they can justify this, often very convincingly, on the grounds of changed expectations and changed intentions. But another, seldom stated, reason may be a wish to 'clear the decks', and blame their predecessors for whatever losses result from asset write-offs. Moreover, amounts written off in the first year will result in corresponding reductions in the amounts which would otherwise have had to have been deducted as expenses in computing profits in future years. Conservatism in the balance sheet results in lack of conservatism in future income statements. Thus large write-offs in the first year result in greater profits in the future.

---

[1] Page 800. The editorial adds, 'We must continually ask ourselves: Is choice absolutely essential? Is there not one method which would be generally applicable? If so, would the loss in freedom outweigh the gain in comparability?' It is not, however, 'freedom', in any meaningful sense of that concept, which is really at stake.

Furthermore, write-offs in the first year reduce the equity base on which return on investment will be calculated in future years. Thus early write-offs of this kind increase the numerator and reduce the denominator of future return on investment calculations and it would be an unusual management that did not feel tempted by this formula after a successful take-over.

Indeed, management does not even have to be changed for such procedures to be attractive. As we saw on page 117, the management of Cunard followed the procedure when they wrote nearly £10 million off the Queen Elizabeth 2. The reinforcing effect of this procedure on the numerator and denominator of future return on investment calculations is obvious.

Not only are management attitudes difficult to measure, it would be very dangerous to use them as a justification for particular methods of valuation since they could equally well be used to justify either extreme conservatism on the one hand, or unwarranted optimism on the other, in making valuations and income measurements. Something more than the assertions of management about the subjective condition of their states of mind seems to be necessary as a basis for the valuations appearing in the accounts presented to shareholders and other investors.

Consistency: a Tool not a Principle

And in fact, as we have emphasised throughout this book, the public interest is involved in all aspects of the activities of the modern corporation; not least in the manner in which corporations, or rather their management, report on the financial results of their activities. It is not in the public interest that management should enjoy such wide freedom of choice in selection of accounting principles when this results in the production of financial reports that are virtually useless to parties who have a clearly defined and legitimate interest in using them.

Nor, in the sham conflict between flexibility and uniformity, can too high a value be placed on the supposed virtue of consistency. Consistency is merely a tool, not a principle, and if it is combined with bad principles it can perpetuate absurdities. Thus a management which is anxious to show good results, or to avoid showing poor results, could well be tempted to capitalise items which should properly be written off; or even to defer the recognition of losses, perhaps capitalising them as assets! Such a policy would be bad enough if it were followed on a once-for-all basis for just one year. But if the 'principle' of consistency is invoked to perpetuate the situation the accounts will become continuously misleading, and consistently wrong.

To put the argument in another form, too much emphasis on consistency results in a degree of uniformity far worse than that advocated by the so-called opponents of 'flexibility'!

The grotesque quality of the offspring of the marriage between multiplicity and consistency was demonstrated by Michael Greener in an interesting article published in the 4 October 1969 issue of *The Accountant*. Mr. Greener analysed the recent reports of twenty-five major companies to see what methods were used in treatment of investment grants (*see* Chapter 12, page 115), and the methods used in computing depreciation and valuing stocks and work-in-progress. (Some indication of the random choice available in these last two areas has already been given above in Chapter 10.) Not only did Mr. Greener find a wide variety of methods used in these three areas, he also discovered that major firms of auditors were apparently quite willing to countenance wide variations in treatments by different clients, even though, as Mr. Greener says, 'it would seem reasonable that one (auditing) firm should speak with one voice'. The argument which would probably be advanced by these firms, that the different treatments are justified by the differing circumstances of their respective clients, is largely negated by the findings of the Scottish Institute's Research Study (*see* page 94 above).

More research of this kind is necessary in this country, and its results should be published widely. The confidentiality which attends so much of the auditor's work (much of it unjustified) acts as a brake on progress; it is therefore all the more important that whatever evidence *is* publicly available should be sifted and collated and analysed, as Mr. Greener has done, but regularly and on a much wider scale. Perhaps one reason why the public in North America is better informed on these matters is because the professional bodies in the United States and Canada take pains to conduct a very careful comparative analysis of the annual accounts of the major companies in their respective countries. The American

Institute's report, *Accounting Trends and Techniques*, which has been published annually for the last twenty-two years, covers the accounts of 600 major U.S. corporations; the equivalent Canadian report covers 325 large Canadian corporations. The English Institute could well sponsor or engage in a similar type of analysis of say the top 400 United Kingdom corporations. Whilst such an analysis might help to arm the profession's critics, in the long run it could only result in an improvement in accounting standards in this country.

The Need for Comparability

For we have to recognise that the quality of financial accounts is a matter of wide public interest, and if we consider for a moment the purpose of financial accounts, so far as investors are concerned, it may help to resolve the dilemma which seems to face us. The main purpose today of published financial accounts is surely to supply investors and potential investors with periodic financial information relevant to their needs in making decisions whether to buy, to sell, or to hold securities in a given company. Other interested parties will also make use of published financial accounts, but their needs are not paramount, and if they differ materially from those of investors and potential investors they should be met by separate types of report. (This is already done, for example, in the case of tax returns filed with the Department of Inland Revenue.) Government and private economists, for example, are keenly interested in the information contained in published accounts, but there is ample reason to believe that if reforms, such as the use of current values in place of historical costs, were instituted the needs of the economists would be much better met than they are at present.

The above outline of the purpose of published financial accounts seems unexceptionable. Yet one has only to compare it with the pronouncements of the English Institute quoted at the beginning of this Chapter to see that its acceptance would involve a drastic shift in the thinking of the professional accounting bodies in this country. Readers of financial accounts are no longer merely interested in liquidity; they are much more concerned with *values* and *earnings prospects* of the companies in which they are interested. That is to say, they are not really interested in a conservative statement of absolute position. They want to make comparisons. These consist of comparisons between the current position and performance of a given company with its position and performance over a series of preceding years; and comparisons of these trends in position and performance of the one company with trends in position and performance of other companies in which the investor is also interested. The need for the first type of comparison makes it perfectly sensible for accountants to insist on the importance of consistency. But the fact that consistency is not the panacea, and that other considerations are important, becomes clear when we consider comparisons of the second type—i.e. inter-company comparisons. Because the investor wants to make comparisons of the second type he becomes concerned with the need for accountants 'to make like things look alike, and unlike things look different', to quote the words of Robert Trueblood, a former president of the American Institute and a senior partner in the international firm of Touche Ross.[2]

Many accountants have argued that such a goal is unattainable in accounting since no two accounting situations are ever exactly alike. To argue this way is a counsel of despair, and ignores achievements in other fields where the intellectual difficulties of correlation and rationalisation are at least as difficult as they are in accounting. Astronomers and biologists, physicists and doctors, lawyers and engineers, are all faced with fields of knowledge in which no two items or situations are ever exactly alike. But it is only the beginning of knowledge in any of these fields to identify and describe the differences which exist. The next, and much more important, step is to classify and organise and arrange this knowledge in such a way that similarities are identified and stressed; this almost invariably involves the intellectual process of abstraction, and it is only by following such a process that the human mind is able to make sense out of its environment. It is this technique of harnessing logic to experience that leads to generalisations such as 'principles' or 'theorems' or 'laws' which, when determined, can be used for the benefit of mankind. To deny that such a process can improve (or perhaps one should say *produce*) a body of accounting principles would be to rank the intellectual qualities of accountants at a level

---

[2] In a paper presented to a conference at the University of Chicago. See *Empirical Research in Accounting: Selected Studies 1966* (Chicago: University of Chicago Press, 1967).

UNIFORMITY OR FLEXIBILITY

not much higher than those of plumbers or carpenters or wallpaperers. Yet calls for reform seem almost inevitably to evoke the spectres of uniformity, the 'rigid set of rules', the 'straitjacket'.

But uniformity, properly understood, is no spectre. Uniformity, in our context, does not mean eliminating alternatives by fiat, sweeping away all but one of the 'rules' in each of the various areas where different alternatives are now available. Uniformity means the establishment of a uniform set of fundamental objectives and concepts governing the nature, the purpose, and the content of published financial accounts; concepts with which any given procedure must be consistent.

Thus accountants need to define the nature and function of financial accounts, and they have to do so in relation to the needs of the persons using these accounts. At present, as the quotations at the beginning of the chapter indicated, accountants have produced a set of arbitrary and often irrelevant rules which produce accounts that are offered to investors, and other users, on a take-it-or-leave-it basis. This is surely putting the cart before the horse. What is needed first of all is to determine, by a carefully organised programme of research, the various categories of user of financial accounts and the needs of users in each category. Only then can the purpose and the nature of the accounts themselves be defined. In addition, there are a number of other fundamental issues which have to be resolved, including the nature of income, the concept of value, the nature of an accounting entity, the nature of an accounting transaction, etc. These must also be researched and resolved in a manner which is relevant to the needs of the users of the accounts.[3]

If this is done (and little attempt has yet been made to deal with this problem in the United Kingdom) it will then be possible to prescribe procedures to implement the defined objectives. There will still be enormous scope for the exercise of experience and judgement by accountants, since problems of measurement, estimation, and allocation (to mention only a few) will remain. Some of these problems can never, by their nature, be resolved deterministically since they involve estimates of what will happen in the future. Even measurements which do not require a crystal ball will still demand the exercise of judgement. Thus, for example, many accounting

---
[3] See Chapter 15. See also the extracts quoted earlier (pp. 111–112) from my letter to Mr. Leach.

intellectuals would support the adoption of replacement cost as a substitute for historical cost in determining asset values.[4] If research and subsequent debate should result in the accountancy profession accepting replacement cost accounting as a basis for measurement, there would still be a great deal of scope for flexibility and judgement in making the required measurements. As an example, the estimates and approximations which would be necessary in determining the replacement cost of fixed assets, such as factory buildings, office buildings, machinery and equipment, etc. would call for qualities of experience and judgement of the highest order.

Thus uniformity does not imply a strait-jacket; it simply means a uniformity of understanding of the nature and purpose of financial accounts, and uniformity of criteria in making selections between possible alternatives. This type of uniformity, combined with a full disclosure of *all* relevant facts is what is required if accounting is to keep pace with the needs of the modern investor. The alternative, exemplified by the present system, is a more or less random stabbing in the dark, a process unguided by any set of rational, consistent objectives.

In such a scheme consistency would remain a virtue, but instead of being applied to procedures and their application it would be applied in developing the set of objectives, and in establishing criteria which would be mutually consistent within themselves. If the objectives and the criteria are properly researched and formulated in the first place, they will leave scope for adaptation to changing circumstances, so that rules can be modified when necessary in a manner consistent with the objectives and the criteria, thereby maintaining the relevance of accounts to the needs of users.

Some Pitfalls to Avoid

It has been suggested in some quarters that since the investor is really interested in the future, the way to solve his difficulties is to require management to formulate and publish their plans and

---

[4] The question of whether 'current values' should be used in published financial accounts has been dealt with at length in a number of academic books and articles. It is of prime importance, and must be considered in depth by the English Institute as part of the Research Programme recommended in the next Chapter. Not all academic accountants support the use of replacement cost as the most appropriate 'current value'; *see,* for example

expectations. While such proposals have the merit of recognising the essential importance of the future so far as the investor is concerned, they are largely impractical. This is partly because they are impossible to verify on an *ex ante* basis, for obvious reasons, and they are therefore likely to be even less credible than *unaudited* conventional accounts. It is true that short-run estimates are quickly corroborated (or otherwise) by circumstances—i.e. by *ex post* comparison with what actually happened. But such *ex post* comparisons are of no value at all in the case of long run estimates since by the time they become possible they are too late to be of any use. Moreover it will never be possible, on either an *ex post* or an *ex ante* basis, to determine to what extent errors in estimates are attributable to honest errors in forecasting and to what extent they are due to a deliberate attempt on the part of management to mislead the readers of the accounts. With all of this in mind one cannot help but feel that such a solution would quickly lead to a complete destruction of faith on the part of the public in all financial accounts.

And it seems futile to launch into an area where deterministic measurements are clearly impossible (because one is dealing with the future), while neglecting the fact that we have yet to solve the much simpler problem of measuring, to the satisfaction of the average investor, what is supposed to have happened in the past.

We should also eschew the temptation to seek uniformity by a process of consensus. One of the deficiencies of the phrase 'generally accepted accounting principles' is its implication that they represent a lowest common denominator. One is not looking for the most popular principles, one is seeking the *best* principles, even if in the early stages such principles are only supported by a minority. Once again, it would be a counsel of despair to argue that a lowest common denominator type of principle is all we can ever hope to achieve; this attitude did not silence Galileo and it should not deter the accounting profession from seeking improvements in the principles of accountancy.

Nor, as we have argued above, will a *laissez faire* approach towards

---

the writings of Professor R. J. Chambers of the University of Sydney, especially his *Accounting, Evaluation and Economic Behaviour* (Englewood Cliffs: Prentice-Hall, 1966) *passim*. Reference should also be made to E. O. Edwards and P. W. Bell, *The Theory and Measurement of Business Income* (Berkeley: University of California Press, 1961), especially Chapter 3.

the evolution of accounting principles work either. Gresham's Law is much too powerful a force in this area, and for accountants to rely on a passive approach to the solution of these problems would be a denial of their professional responsibilities to the public, and would postpone reform to the Greek Kalends.

Nor will the solution be found by the piecemeal process of attending to problems as and when they arise. Nor can it be found by a combination of such 'firefighting methods' combined with periods of reflective activity in which attempts are made to generalise the accumulation of piecemeal solutions. Such a process is almost entirely random, and lacks any fundamental intellectual or conceptual roots since it operates on an unplanned and unstructured basis. It is attractive to some practitioners since it results in a show of activity, and problems apparently get solved. But without any integrating structure of fundamental principles or objectives, the ensuing goulash of 'solutions' which emerges has little if any internal consistency and, as an inspection of the English Institute's Recommendations will reveal, the 'solutions' themselves tend to be unsupported by any corpus of consistent reasoning and logic.

In conclusion it should be emphasised that the issue of uniformity versus flexibility is a false one. No sensible accountant can be content with the present 'flexible' situation; and no sensible accountant wants to replace it with a strait-jacket. The issue is not uniformity *or* flexibility, the need is for uniformity *and* flexibility. A suggested programme for achieving this object is given in Chapter 15.

15

Proposals for Reform

It should now be apparent that a number of things are seriously wrong with the current state of accounting practice. Most, if not all, of the deficiencies cannot be remedied without devoting serious and sustained attention to the underlying, fundamental, theoretical problems. This book is not an academic treatise, and it certainly does not constitute an attempt to produce final solutions to the issues discussed. It should in fact be clear by now that the solutions will not be found easily; if this could be done the problems could scarcely be regarded as difficult, and they would have been solved long ago.

But it would be unreasonable, and unfair, to criticise the accounting profession for its unsolved problems without at the same time offering suggestions as to how the problems should be tackled. The purpose of this chapter is to offer some proposals for reform.

What is Needed

The first thing that has to be done is to define the nature of the problem, preferably in teleological terms by describing the ultimate need or objective.

If we can accept that the main purpose of financial accounts of public companies is to serve the needs of investors, both large and small, then it seems clear that financial accounts should be produced in a form which provides information relevant to the needs of such investors. In a larger sense one can say that the purpose of financial accounts is to provide information relevant to the needs of users. Whatever our prescription, it must define the needs to be served and it can only do this by defining *whose* needs are to be served.

That, logically, is the first step, but it is only the beginning. It is then necessary for financial accountants to develop a well integrated structure of accounting theory and practice. Such a structure, if properly researched and carefully thought out, will meet the ultimate objective by providing practical rules and procedures which will be based upon a theoretical foundation of carefully researched objectives of financial reporting, supported by a set of self-consistent concepts covering the whole basis of measurement of costs, values, and income.

In developing this structure it will be essential to distinguish between conceptual problems and measurement problems.

Conceptual problems deal with such matters as:
  (a) the relevance of different kinds of cost calculations to the needs of users.
  (b) the nature of the concept of 'value' which is most relevant to the needs of users. For example, does it make sense to prepare balance sheets on the basis of historical cost? If not, why not, and what is the best alternative?
  (c) what is the most relevant concept of income, so far as the users of published financial accounts are concerned? What are the implications of this concept when considering items (a) and (b) above? And vice versa.
  (d) numerous other difficulties, such as the problem of income tax allocation, the problem of investment grants, the price level problem, etc. Although in a sense they can be regarded as subsidiary to the problems defined in items (a), (b), and (c) (at least in the logical sense) they are nevertheless important in their own right.

Measurement problems are of great importance, and often of great complexity. Their solution often calls, and will continue to call, for experience and judgement of the highest order. Measurement problems can be extremely vexing even when they deal with past transactions—particularly where questions of allocation are involved. Measurement problems are even more difficult when they involve judgements and estimates about the future. But, perplexing as the problems of accounting measurement can be, we must not overlook the fact that they occupy a role junior to that of the conceptual problems. This is for the simple and apparently obvious, yet frequently overlooked, reason that even the most skilfully executed measurement is of little value if one has not first of all defined with precision exactly what it is that one is trying to measure. The practising accountant, possibly because he is so continuously and intimately involved with measurement problems, often overlooks this fact.

Who should Solve the Problem

Most, if not all, intelligent accountants in this country seem ready to accept that there *is* a serious problem and that it must be solved. If this point is accepted, we must next consider by whom the problem should be solved. Several possibilities spring to mind.

PARLIAMENT AND THE PROFESSION

The English Institute frequently voices the opinion that improvements in accounting can best be achieved by having Parliament tighten up the Companies Act on the basis of recommendations put forward by the Institute (and by other interested parties such as the Stock Exchange). This idea has been discussed earlier in Chapters 11 and 13. The reasons are understandable; without statutory backing many auditors feel that they are unable to enforce recommendations of the professional bodies against the wishes of management. But the solution surely entails jumping out of the frying pan and into the fire. Defining accounting principles, or even rules and procedures, by Act of Parliament is surely the most rigid and inflexible method one can imagine. It delivers the job of framing the final definition into the hands of parliamentary draughtsmen and legislators (who have no obvious expertise in accountancy) and it makes the job of amendment and modification an extremely difficult and arduous one. Moreover, since the Act cannot be interpreted by reference to the debate which took place in Parliament, but only by a strict interpretation of its printed words, a large degree of inflexibility is introduced even at the very beginning when the Act is passed. Thus, the English Institute already finds it necessary to obtain and publish counsel's opinions on the legal interpretation of various clauses in the Companies Act.

For these reasons, and because the matter involves at least a partial abdication of responsibility by the profession, this method ought to be rejected.

A BRITISH S.E.C.

Although a British SEC, presumably set up as a government agency along the lines of the American SEC, would be less bureaucratic in its implications than a more extensive use of the Companies Act, it seems clearly undesirable to have the job of defining accounting principles handed over, unilaterally, to a government agency. This method will therefore not be discussed any further.

However, the alternative of setting up a British SEC with the object of leaving it to ride herd on the accounting profession by arming it with reserve powers is perhaps worth some consideration. It will be recalled that the American SEC was given sweeping powers by Congress, in 1933 and subsequently, entitling it to prescribe accounting procedures, rules, etc. In practice the SEC has been very sparing in the use of these powers, and has preferred to leave it to the American Institute to look after these matters. However, as we have seen, the presence of the SEC in the background galvanised the American Institute into action, and it has been running ever since. From this point of view, it might be worthwhile to have a British SEC to perform the same function on the British profession.

There are two arguments against doing this. In the first place, there is the fact that the English Institute has recently issued its Statement of Intent to Advance Accounting Standards in the 1970s, 'improving substantially the comparability and usefulness of financial statements, and providing users of accounts with the information which they want'. Unless the Institute falls down on the job, it does not seem reasonable to superimpose an SEC at this time. Secondly, the possibility that an SEC might be formed in the future is likely to be almost as effective an instrument of gentle persuasion as forming such a body immediately, if it were intended that the body, once formed, would hold its powers in reserve.

For these reasons it seems sensible to hold the idea of an SEC in abeyance, at least so far as its role in the determination of accounting principles is concerned.

MANAGEMENT

This possibility need not delay us for long. It has been explained in earlier chapters how management has set most of the rules in the past, with the professional accountant taking a relatively passive role. It is this situation, more than anything else, which has given rise to the proliferation of 'accounting principles'. It seems absurd that management should be cast in the role of an actor who is entitled to 'write his own reviews'. Clearly, if the situation is to be improved the profession must play the dominant role.

THE PROFESSION

It should be clear from what has been said above, and in earlier chapters, that it is the profession which should have the exclusive responsibility for defining, promulgating, and enforcing accounting principles. If the profession is to do this successfully it will have to make a realistic attempt to tackle the independence problem dealt with in Chapter 13, and it will undoubtedly need some statutory backing (as described later). But there seems no doubt that the principles of accountancy are the responsibility of the accounting profession. The only question that really needs to be settled in the United Kingdom is the question of 'Which professional body?' Whatever the fate of the proposals for the integration of the several professional accounting bodies, the choice would seem to lie between the English and the Scottish Institutes, or both.

It is very odd that the Scottish Institute, which is the oldest professional accounting body in the world, has taken a rearguard position on the question of definition of accounting principles. It is all the more surprising since Scottish chartered accountants are so proud of their academic and intellectual quality. A professional accounting body with these traditions, even such a relatively small professional accounting body, might have been expected to have been in the vanguard in giving intellectual leadership in the determination of accounting principles in this country.

Yet in fact, as this book has made plain, it has been the English Institute which has led the way, and which has, accordingly, come in for all of the criticism. 'Uneasy lies the head that wears the crown'! This fact clearly gives the English Institute precedence, and there seems little doubt that it will be the body which will shoulder the responsibility in the future. The cooperation of the Scottish Institute will doubtless be welcomed, if they wish to participate, but it seems unlikely that at this stage they can expect to be treated as anything more than a very junior partner. Had they been the first in the field the story might have been completely different.

The English Institute's Plans

This book has been critical of the English Institute, and with good reason. It has had in the past a squirearchical manner about it which at times has brought it to the verge of ossification.

Some of this has been evident in some of the reactions to recent criticism. But the winds of change have been blowing through the Institute's headquarters in the past few months and, under the leadership of Mr. Leach, its president, the Institute has reacted to the criticism with commendable swiftness by publishing its Statement of Intent on Accounting Standards in the 1970s. This Statement proclaims the Institute's intention to advance accounting standards along the following lines:

(1) narrowing the areas of difference and variety in accounting practice
(2) disclosure of accounting bases
(3) disclosure of departures from established definitive accounting standards
(4) wider exposure for major new proposals on accounting standards
(5) continuing programme for encouraging improved accounting standards in legal and regulatory measures.

This declaration represents a big step forward. One can criticise its reliance on extensions to companies legislation, its apparent emphasis on an *ad hoc* programme of reform, its failure to mention the problem of independence, and the fact that it does not mention a need to disclose the monetary effect of departures from established accounting standards. (Indeed, it would be interesting to know how the monetary effect of such departures *could* be measured when there are so many different extant standards to be departed from!) One can also perhaps lament the fact that when the president states, in his covering letter, that 'The Council's new proposals will not succeed without the collective support of our non-practising and practising members and the cooperation of industry, finance and commerce', he appears to overlook the possibility of an intellectual contribution by the academic community.

It is easy, however, to criticise; what is really important about the Statement of Intent is the fact that it has been made and that things will never be the same again in British accountancy. The English Institute has stood up and declared itself foursquare for progress and improvement, and it deserves the greatest possible credit for having done so.

The remainder of this Chapter will be concerned with some proposals about the way in which improvements can be made.

The Approach of the Scientist

This is not the place to engage in pseudo-philosophical discussion about whether accountancy is an art or a science. Like economics, it is possibly a bit of both; a science when it turns out right, and an art when it turns out wrong.

But we accountants can learn something from observing the manner in which the scientist organises and develops his discipline. Arguments by analogy between professions, or between disciplines, must be evaluated with care. Nevertheless, there is much about the approach of the scientist which is relevant when we consider what is the best way of developing accounting principles.

To begin with, science and scientists have objectives. In essence these consist of a desire to seek the truth and explain the world. 'Truth' and 'explanations' are in one sense absolute. They are also, in another sense, peculiar to the needs of the particular scientific discipline. But in the last analysis the work of the scientist cannot be understood without first of all understanding his objectives.

'Scientific Method' is a term which is often used to describe the way in which scientists go about their work. The Method consists essentially of the accumulation of facts and data, by experiment and observation; the organisation of the facts and data into groups by a process of classification; the formulation of 'hypotheses' to account for the facts and to explain their interrelationships; the formulation of a hypothesis is not a deductive process, it involves an imaginative 'inductive' leap in the dark; the validity of the hypothesis is then tested empirically by a further experiment or observation; generally speaking, the testing process consists of using the hypothesis to predict some new fact or relationship and then attempting to verify the accuracy of the prediction by experiment or observation; hypotheses which survive a sufficient number of tests eventually become elevated to the status of theories; hypotheses which fail their tests are discarded, or are modified and re-tested.

It can be seen why science has been defined as 'organised common sense'. At the same time, one can appreciate that 'organised common sense' can involve enormous degrees of intellectual subtlety and complexity.

Science, in the form described above, might be regarded as 'pure', as distinct from 'applied'. But much of the distinction between pure and applied science is artificial, based in large part on a form of intellectual snobbery. (This point has been well brought out by Sir Peter Medawar in his essay 'Two Conceptions of Science' published in his book *The Art of the Soluble* (London, Methuen 1967) (pp. 113–128; also pp. 11–14).) The analogy with accountancy is, if you like, between theory and practice. Scientific theories form the basis of practical rules which are used by men in such varied occupations as designing and building bridges, weather prediction, practising medicine, growing wheat, and flying to the moon.

Similarly, a soundly constructed theory of accountancy will find immediate practical application in meeting the objectives defined earlier in this Chapter, and throughout this book.

A Programme for the Profession

What is offered here is a proposal for an integrated programme of research which, although it will certainly not solve all our problems, will set the profession well on the way to meeting the needs of users of published financial accounts.

DEFINITION OF OBJECTIVES

The profession should take immediate steps to promote research into the objectives of financial accounting. Clearly, a considerable amount of field work will be necessary in the form of surveys, interviews, etc. The research should attempt to define with precision who are the users of published financial accounts and what are their needs. The needs of the users will have to be defined in relation to the type of decisions that users can reasonably be expected to wish to make on the basis of published financial accounts. Having determined what the various classes of users are, and the decisions which they are attempting to make, it will be possible to deduce the type of information which they need. This sets the framework against which one can define the objectives of published financial accounts and the type of information which they should contain. Whether such information is obtainable, and if it is not, what is the best possible substitute, are questions which will be dealt with later in the programme.

TERMINOLOGY

A feature of current financial accounting and reporting which bedevils expert and layman alike is the welter of ambiguity which clouds and confuses the meaning of almost every term used by the accountant. The situation has arisen partly because the world of corporate finance, with which accountants deal, grows daily more complex, and partly because accountants have seldom tried to get down to first principles in defining their concepts (which makes it hardly surprising that the terms they use are woolly). The English Institute should therefore establish a committee, supported by a research programme, in order to attempt to define with clarity and precision the meaning of such commonly used terms as 'true and fair view', 'income', 'asset', 'goodwill', etc. The task sounds simple; in fact it will be found to be immensely complex and it should be a fertile seedbed for other research projects of a more fundamental nature.

DATA COLLECTION ON CURRENT PRACTICE

As noted earlier in Chapter 14, there has been little attempt in this country to collect, codify, and publish details of accounting presentation and procedures of major British companies. Reference was made to the American publication, *Accounting Trends and Techniques*, and the corresponding Canadian publication, *Financial Reporting in Canada*. The English Institute should act immediately to establish a similar programme in Britain, and the results of this effort should be published annually. This will provide a great deal of factual information which can be used by the profession in promoting an improvement in standards of accounting presentation and disclosure. Without the necessary facts, carefully collected and analysed, it is difficult if not impossible to make a serious effort at improvement.

INDEPENDENCE OF THE AUDITOR

The question of the auditor's independence is one which the profession cannot continue to ignore, or to attempt to smother by pretending to confuse it with the question of integrity and crying 'foul'. Nor can it be ducked by arguing that the professional accountant runs the risk of an action for negligence if he commits an error of judgement. The present confused state of accounting principles leaves room for such wide margins of error that such risks are relatively small at the present time. The risks will undoubtedly increase in the future, as accounting principles are improved, and so will the need for auditors to be seen to be independent. Moreover, whilst auditors may suffer some risks, investors suffer much larger risks in many cases. Such investors are unlikely to be convinced by what must seem to be hypothetical claims on the part of the auditor. (Particularly if the auditor is not, in fact, sued for negligence.)

The problem of independence is a very serious one, and it is not likely to go away. It is a time bomb ticking away underneath the seat of the profession, and the sooner the profession faces up to the problem and solves it the safer the profession will be in future controversies.

THE PROBLEM OF 'TEETH'

It has been argued above that it is a mistake for the accounting profession to look to Parliament to enshrine, and ultimately fossilise, its accounting principles by turning them into statutes. At the same time it is quite legitimate for the profession to look to Parliament for support in enforcing principles which have been defined. Surely the right and proper way is for the profession to ask Parliament to write a clause into the Companies Act stating that 'accounting principles and procedures' shall be those defined from time to time by the English Institute, and currently in effect. Such a procedure would give the full force of law to accounting principles, and it would also ensure that full control over the definition, amendment, and evolution of accounting principles was placed squarely in the hands of the profession—where it belongs. If we deserve, and if we wish to be regarded as a great profession, then we must be prepared to take into our own hands the responsibility for defining and promulgating accounting principles. And we should ask Parliament to give us the authority to do this and the power to enforce it.

FULL DISCLOSURE

The fundamental problems of financial accounting theory and practice will not be solved quickly. It may take ten or more years to do the job properly. In the meantime, the profession should make it absolutely clear that it is fully committed to the principle of full disclosure, and it should be prepared to accept the operational consequences of such a commitment.

PROPOSALS FOR REFORM

This means (*see* Appendices I and III) that companies should be required to define in detail the accounting principles, procedures and practices that are used by them and which form the foundation for their published financial accounts. It is not necessary that all these details should 'clutter up' the annual report. They can be filed with the Registrar, and made available for inspection at any time. In this way any interested party would be able to obtain the information required. This is elaborated upon in Appendix III.

Furthermore, companies should be required to show, in respect of each item on their balance sheet and each item in their statement of profit and loss, the highest and the lowest figures which would have been calculated for that item had the two extreme sets of generally accepted accounting principles been used in valuation. In addition, of course, the company would show in the body of the balance sheet or income statement the actual figure which they had arrived at by the methods or principles which they in fact selected.

It can be argued that it would be difficult to calculate and supply this information. So it might; but surely this is no argument against producing information which is certainly of very considerable interest and relevance to the needs of investors. It might also be argued that the extremities would be so far apart that the investor would be confused. This is also quite possibly true; all the more need to get to work quickly to 'narrow the areas of difference'. And nothing will be better calculated to silence the complacent than a revelation of just how wide apart the extremities really are.

But, surely the conclusive argument must be that if the accountant professes to believe in 'full disclosure' then he is obliged to practise what he preaches?

AN ACCOUNTING PRINCIPLES BOARD

A general description of the American Institute's Accounting Principles Board, and its origins, has been given in Chapter 11. As a pragmatic attempt to achieve a general improvement in the quality of accounting principles, as they are applied in practice, this seems to be an eminently sensible institution. The Americans have had sufficient experience with it to have 'debugged' the operation, and the English Institute could set up a Committee to consider whether or not such a Board should be established in this country. The English Institute's committee should be required to produce a report, which would be published, explaining its reasons for or against such a move.

AN ACCOUNTING COURT

Several possible variations are available here, and they are described in Appendix III. The arguments in favour of such a procedure are presented in this Appendix, and they will not be repeated here. Once again, the English Institute should set up a committee to investigate this whole matter and report back; with the report being published, and giving reasons in favour of its decision. At the very least, the Institute's Professional Standards Committee should be given more 'teeth', both in dealing with bad practice and in encouraging and supporting good practice by the independent public accountant.

A RESEARCH FOUNDATION

This is possibly the most important requirement of all, if the British profession is to develop a set of accounting principles and procedures which have solid intellectual and theoretical foundations. The American Institute has had such a body for the last ten years or so, and the Australians have recently got their Research Foundation (a cooperative endeavour between the Australian Society and the Australian Institute) into full swing. The English Institute should take immediate steps to form a similar body in this country. It should be supplied with a full-time Director, supported by adequate full-time secretarial and research staff. The Director, in the initial stages at least, should look to the intellectuals in the profession, and to the universities, for most of the assistance he will need. In later stages it ought to be possible, as in the United States, to staff the Research Foundation with full-time and high-powered research men of its own.

The activity of the Research Foundation would be in part coordinating; that is to say, it would bring together and draw very heavily upon the fact-finding research activities outlined in the paragraphs above. As in science it is impossible to conduct intelligent research in accounting without the basic data. However, it should be the ultimate objective of the Research Foundation to develop a consistent and coherent body of accounting theory, and, by participating actively behind the scenes in the work of the Accounting Principles Board, ensure that theoretical considerations form the bedrock upon which future practical recommendations are built. The Research Foundation would also give assistance to the Court (or to the strengthened Professional Standards Committee) in dealing with day-to-day practical problems of application of accounting recommendations and procedures.

Fees

The English Institute at the present time is scarcely paying its way. In its latest annual report it was estimated that there would be a deficit of at least £100,000 in the 1969 financial year. If integration with the Association of Certified and Corporate Accountants, the Institute of Cost and Works Accountants, and the Institute of Municipal Treasurers and Accountants, goes through as planned the increase in administrative and other costs should be exceeded by the increase in the income. However, this surplus (if it materialises) has no doubt already been spoken for. If the profession is to make a really effective onslaught upon the accounting principles problem in the 1970s it will have to allocate a very substantial sum of money to the process. Nor, in the nature of things, can this be a once-and-for-all process; it will be a continuing one and its annual cost will no doubt increase steadily as the years go by. It therefore seems that the Institute must increase its fees in order to deal with this problem. Perhaps the amount earmarked for these activities should be specified, so that members know exactly how much of their fees are being spent on education and research activities.

A costly programme of this kind will no doubt evoke strong protest, particularly from the backwoodsmen. This should not deter the leaders of the Institute. The alternative to having the profession doing this job, and paying for it out of fees, is to have the government do it, paying for it out of taxes. In the short run this might seem a cheaper way from the point of view of the individual member; in the long run it would be the most expensive way for the profession to deal with these problems.

Academic Participation

If the British accounting profession is to achieve any real success in solving the problems described in this book it seems clear that it will require substantial assistance from the academic community. This is apparent not only from the nature of the problems but also from a consideration of the way they have been tackled overseas. As noted earlier, on page 146, it is not yet obvious that this is fully appreciated by the English Institute. This no doubt is partly due to the fact that British academic accountants have been few in number, and relatively inactive in developing the theoretical aspects of financial accounting.

Unlike the lawyers and the doctors, the accountants have not succeeded in persuading the British universities, or the University Grants Committee, that the practice of their profession is rooted in an academic discipline which ought to be much more strongly represented in the universities. Urgent steps must be taken to remedy this situation if the profession is to develop as it should. Some concrete proposals about what to do in this area are contained in my article 'The Need for Lond-Range Planning in Developing Educational Policy for the Profession', published in the January 1970 issue of *The Accountant's Magazine*.

It is not so long ago since Britain led the world in pure and applied science; this was in the days when brainpower, unaccompanied by vast amounts of capital, was enough. It is no longer enough in many fields of technology, but there is no reason why it should not suffice in the field of accountancy. We do not need very large sums of money to provide the remedies suggested in this book. All we really need is a relatively small change in the way in which the profession allocates its resources, combined with a very large change in the way in which the profession looks at some of its problems.

The time to make these changes is now.

Appendix 1

Article by Professor Stamp (11 September 1969), a Reply by Mr. R. G. Leach (22 September 1969), and a letter from Professor Stamp (26 September 1969), published in *The Times Business News*. (Reprinted by permission of *The Times*.)

(a) Article by Professor Stamp (published 11 September 1969)

Auditing the Auditors

The Pergamon affair has thrown fresh light on a number of problems which are facing, and which ought to be faced by the accounting profession in this country. The fact that yet another leading City firm of chartered accountants is now to be called in will no doubt cause some to ask, *'Quis custodiet ipsos custodes?'* Or, in the vernacular of the marketplace, who will audit the auditors? And the Government's interest in the whole subject of auditing and approving profit forecasts has clearly been aroused.

For the Pergamon affair is not the first occasion on which warning signals have been run up. One has only to think of Sir Frank Kearton's complaints to the President of the Institute of Chartered Accountants in 1968 about the multiplicity of 'generally accepted accounting principles' and the problems this generates in reconciling different accountants' measures of profit and value; or the wide differences between accountants revealed in the differences between the A.E.I. forecasts and the results. In both these cases, and in others here and overseas, serious doubt has been cast on the usefulness, let alone the theoretical validity, of the figures prepared and 'authenticated' by accountants.

There are in fact several related matters which deserve to engage the attention of the profession and the public. I shall deal with them in turn and, at the end of this article, suggest some obvious reforms.

In the first place there is the deceptive nature of the phrase 'accounting principles'. The word principle lends a spurious air of authority and accuracy to a situation which is in fact almost chaotic. As the Pergamon case has shown, accountants find it exceedingly difficult to agree upon or apply the 'principles' to be used in amortising development expenditures, treating transactions between related members of a group of companies, valuing stocks, or determining at what point income can be said to have been earned. There are many other areas that are equally contentious.

In all cases it is the principles as well as the practice that are in conflict, and it is little use to argue that 'judgment' must be the deciding factor, when the judgment of so many leading firms of accountants is so clearly in conflict. Medical practice is based on judgment but it is also based on principles with a sound theoretical foundation. This is not so in the case of accounting, and most of the accountant's so-called principles are merely descriptions of current or, even worse, past, practice; rules which in many cases were drawn up on an *ad hoc* basis to deal with the expediencies of a passing moment.

The fact that these rules have in many cases been codified by the Institute of Chartered Accountants should not delude us into thinking that they were drawn up inside any theoretical framework. Indeed, it has been calculated by one authority that the profession has authorised so many different ways of doing the same thing that the rules for valuing the assets on a balance-sheet can be combined together in over a million different ways to produce over a million different 'true and fair views' of the same facts.

This situation will persist so long as the profession regards principles merely as an attempt to describe what is being done in the best firms. This approach may be satisfactory in prescribing the 'principles' of plumbing, or of wallpapering, or of carpentry. It is surely not good enough for a profession which believes itself to be the intellectual equal of the legal and medical professions.

The second problem relates to the functions of the independent auditor. His task is to examine his client company's financial accounts, to decide (behind a cloak of secrecy, and without revealing any of the alternative principles which he has considered) whether the accounts are drawn up in accordance with good accounting principles; and then to report, usually very briefly and without qualification, to the shareholders.

It is extraordinary that a profession which believes in 'full disclosure' reveals so little about what leads it to its belief in the truth and fairness of its clients' accounts. Such a system makes it very difficult for anyone to analyse the accounting decisions which have been taken, or to point out ways in which improvements might be made (as is possible in the case of legal decisions). In a word, it inhibits progress and, by placing a veil around what has been decided and done, it puts a premium on mediocrity and incompetence.

Such a situation would be difficult enough for an auditor if he could be regarded as completely independent in his point of view. But in many cases this is far from so. Thus many auditors are involved with their clients in other capacities—as tax consultants, management consultants, advising on computing installations, etc.

The auditor may even own shares in his client firm, and he is of course paid his fee by his client. Yet once a year, and possibly more frequently, he is called upon to deliver an independent judgment on his client's accounts, a judgment which, as the Pergamon affair demonstrates, can have a decisive effect on the fortunes of his client.

It is simply not good enough for the auditor to answer this with the comment that 'independence is a state of mind'. States of mind, unlike the facts I have cited, cannot be measured objectively. They can be judged by the end result of the auditor's mental processes, but since this is the auditor's opinion on the client's accounts such an assessment would be a question-begging operation at best.

When there are over a million different ways of begging the question it becomes clear that the public interest is seriously involved.

The essence of the independence problem is that the auditor is expected to assume the role of a judge while he lacks many of the important attributes of independence which give authority to the judge in the courts, and which ensure that his judgments will be received with respect.

Judges have no pecuniary or other interest in the parties who appear before them, they are not paid by them, and they do not look to them for security of tenure. The fact that the same cannot be said of the auditor, when he acts as a judge, is surely something which deserves careful attention. The kind of attention, for example, which the medical profession is giving to the problem of deciding when a heart transplant donor is dead. It is not surprising that this is not a judgment which it is felt can be left to the surgeon who is planning to perform the operation.

Having defined some of the problems, let us consider possible solutions.

It is obviously essential for the profession to initiate a full-scale research programme as soon as possible.

Steps in this direction have already been taken in many overseas countries, including Australia and the United States, where it has been recognized that a study of the underlying theoretical concepts is just as important as attempts to define extant practice. The English Institute of Chartered Accountants has a heavy anti-intellectual bias (few of its members are university graduates) which it will have to shed if it really wants to command the respect now enjoyed by its sister professions of law and medicine.

It will take some time, even if a research programme is begun immediately, to produce a set of rational, logical and self-consistent accounting principles.

What can be done in the meantime? The best approach (and this may be necessary for some years) is to require companies to disclose not only their income and balance-sheet values in accordance with the accounting 'principles' which they happen to have chosen, but also the highest and lowest figures in the range of such values which would have been obtained if alternative 'principles' had been used instead.

This will enable the reader to judge the margin of error, or 'difference of judgment', in each case. In addition, companies should be required to define in great detail the precise principles they have in fact used in valuing stocks, computing depreciation, capitalizing assets, recording intercompany transactions, accounting for revenues, providing for bad debts, handling investment grants and all the other areas where more than one alternative is 'generally accepted'.

The independence problem can be dealt with by recognizing that a process of judgment is involved, and that it must be performed by persons who are in fact independent and are seen to be independent.

APPENDIX I

Thus a panel of judges could be established, appointed and paid by the state, whose duty it would be to resolve contentious issues in a way as fair as possible to all the parties involved.

All judgments (unless clearly confidential) would be published, and a body of 'case law' would thus be established and could be used in guiding auditors and judges in the future. Such a system need not result in delays in the issuance of auditors' reports (in fact, British auditors could speed up their work considerably as it is if they applied the modern methods used overseas).

An issue would only be brought before a judge if the auditor felt that it was necessary to have the independent judge's authority behind the auditor's own opinion. The onus would be on the auditor to decide in which cases it was necessary to consult the judge, or, having approached the judge, whether he should accept his ruling. Naturally, failure to consult the judge, or failure to accept his ruling, would be a fact to be taken into account if the client's financial accounts should later be brought into dispute.

This system, and the strengthening of the disclosure requirements recommended above, would do much to speed up the evolution of accounting principles in this country and, by giving auditors the opportunity to obtain authoritative support in their interpretation of principles in contentious areas, it should strengthen the position of the auditor when any open conflict arises.

Other solutions are of course possible; a British Securities and Exchange Commission has been suggested as one necessary reform. In my opinion the degree of regulation which this would entail could well constitute a cure which would be worse than the disease. The S.E.C. was established in response, partly, to a degree of financial chicanery in United States business from which we still seem to be mercifully immune in Britain. But there is no doubt that reforms are needed in Britain, and they are needed now.

It is too early to speak of cleaning the Augean stables. But further neglect will sharpen the analogy, and it should be remembered that when Hercules finally perfomed that task the price he ultimately exacted was very high indeed.

(b) Reply by Mr. R. G. Leach (published 22 September 1969)

Accountants and the Public Interest

A professional answer to Professor Stamp. Ronald Leach, President of the Institute of Chartered Accountants of England and Wales, is replying to an article by Professor Edward Stamp that appeared in Business News on September 11, which was highly critical of the accounting profession.

The accountancy profession welcomes constructive criticism; however certain observations made recently about us, in particular by Professor Edward Stamp (Business News, September 11) call for reply. The tenor of Professor Stamp's article was especially damaging to the British accountancy profession because it suggested that it lacked principle (*sic*), failed to exercise independent judgment, had an archaic outlook, and, at least as regards my own institute, had an 'anti-intellectual bias'. The reader was left with the impression that accountants in this country are a pretty ineffective and inefficient lot.

Before I deal in detail with our critics' points, it is necessary to regain perspective on the standing and quality of the profession in this country by reminding readers of some obvious areas in which my profession operates powerfully for the public interest.

The English institute has produced a series of statements on accounting principles and auditing which are respected and influential throughout the world and which are not only sound but of immense value and benefit to members of the profession, to industry, and to the investing public.

We study all proposals for new legislation in the fields of taxation and company law, and make constructive proposals for change and improvement which are welcomed and seriously considered by the authorities.

We are proceeding with a bold scheme for the development and integration of the profession in the future, including plans for higher educational entry levels, a wider choice of training background, and a broader syllabus. Following our example, similar developments are being considered overseas in countries like Australia and Canada.

We have mustered substantial support and have made significant

APPENDIX I

progress in our campaign to establish means of reviewing and rationalizing the tax system.

We are consulted by the Government on a multitude of matters in which our members give help and advice without reward.

It has been suggested that accountants themselves are confused by a multiplicity of accounting principles. Professor Stamp pleads eloquently for a set of rational, logical and self-consistent accounting principles which, if they are to achieve the aims he desires, must by implication be simple, unambiguous and generally applicable. He implies that the profession, and my institute in particular, have been lacking in diligence and in appreciation of the potential contribution of the academic accountant to these aims.

I know I speak for all accountants in wishing that Professor Stamp's objectives were immediately achievable. I differ from him because in reality the business world is highly complex, diverse and volatile, and I see little prospect of developing simple, unambiguous, generally applicable principles in the short term. Recognizing this situation, the English institute has responded by formulating broad principles which are capable of being applied differently in different circumstances. Professor Stamp seems to hold a similar position, because he has elsewhere said of 'a set of rigid rules' that 'in my view such a cure is likely to be worse than the original disease'.

The real difficulty is not the absence or multitude of accounting principles but applying them to the facts of a particular business. The root of the problem lies in the fact that the assessment of profit of a going concern for so short a period as 12 months is usually not a simple matter of objective recording and calculation; it calls largely for commercial judgment in evaluating the outcome of transactions not yet completed.

It is for management to exercise this judgment; the auditor must satisfy himself that it has been exercised fairly on the basis of reliable and relevant information and of tenable consistent and realistic assumptions. If the auditor is not substantially satisfied, the client either amends his accounts—the normal procedure—or must accept a qualified report.

On what points then would an auditor feel it necessary to refer to Professor Stamp's proposed panel of judges?

As I said, I do not believe that periodic financial statements can be fairly prepared in accordance with rigid rules. The problems can be illustrated by considering what is involved in valuing stock and calculating depreciation, both of which are substantially dependent on the exercise of judgment.

There must always be uncertainty about the realizability of unsold stock. It would be easy enough to establish a rule that stock should be brought into account at a nominal value or at least far below any price it might foreseeably be worth, but this would not satisfy either the shareholders or the Inland Revenue, or, indeed, the true and fair view required by the Companies Acts.

At the start of the takeover movement after the war we saw instances of undervaluation of assets and of consequent damage to shareholders.

If a new management takes control—following a takeover—their general policy as it affects stock valuation may be quite different from their predecessors. They may wish to discontinue or change product lines, alter the product range, or reduce drastically the volume of stock which is carried, with the result that some stocks immediately become redundant or obsolete. This does not in any way imply that the previous valuation was at fault at the time and in the circumstances in which it was made.

Again, it is a generally accepted accounting principle that the cost of machinery should be charged against revenue over the period of the machinery's useful life.

How long this life is likely to be and whether in the circumstances of the particular business the cost should be written off in equal amounts each year or on some other basis are matters of judgment in the light of the nature of the machinery, the probable intensity of its use, the prospects of its becoming obsolete before it is worn out, the probable policy of competitors, and so on. The management of one business may fairly reach one conclusion; that of another business may fairly reach another. Both conclusions will be acceptable provided they are adhered to consistently.

Where I feel in sympathy with Professor Stamp is in his suggestion for fuller disclosure of the accounting methods adopted wherever this is practicable. The 1967 Companies Act already requires the basis of valuation of stock to be stated; further development in this direction seems desirable. On the other hand, care has to be taken not so to clutter up published accounts with notes and explanations that the salient features of the accounts become obscured.

APPENDIX I

I reject absolutely the suggestion that the independence and objectivity of auditors in this country is suspect. The facts that their remuneration is paid out of shareholders' funds and often agreed with the directors, and that auditors may carry out other services for the company are irrelevant unless it is implied that the auditors' duty to report their opinion of the view given by the accounts is affected by these pecuniary considerations.

I do not believe that the manner of their remuneration impairs the honesty and objectivity with which auditors render their professional services, any more than it does that of other professional men in a comparable position, such as lawyers or doctors.

I am not aware of a shred of evidence that members of my profession shirk their duty, and their training is directed to taking an independent and honest view.

Every year countless balance-sheets and prospectuses of public companies are issued: I am not aware of any cases in which an auditor has been accused of lack of independence, although he may in some cases be deceived or less vigilant than he might be. But that is a different matter, and such cases are few and far between.

Professor Stamp's statement that British auditors report 'usually very briefly, and without qualification, to the shareholders' is made to sound like an accusation, as though auditors were failing to do their job. The facts are first, that 'clean' British audit reports are deliberately brief so as to highlight those which contain qualifications, and secondly, as I have previously noted, British managements generally prefer to amend their financial statements rather than receive a qualified audit report. Even so, about one in 40 of quoted companies receive qualified audit reports, though commentators often fail to notice them.

I am sorry that Professor Stamp saw fit to disparage the standards and practice of the British accountancy profession by comparison with the profession overseas. The fact is that the results of authoritative international comparisons of accounting and auditing standards in America, Britain and Canada which are beginning to emerge show how similar they are in philosophy and approach.

It is instructive to compare Professor Stamp's suggestion that British auditors could speed up their work if they applied the 'modern methods used overseas' with the fact that elsewhere in his recent writings he holds up as a model of international comparison the speed with which Marks and Spencer produces its audited financial statements.

The truth is that international comparison shows that the accountancy profession in this country is in the forefront of new thinking and innovatory technique. I come later to our position on profit forecasts.

Our general standards of disclosure of information are probably ahead of world practice as a result of influence wielded by the profession and requirements established by the 1967 Companies Act and the London Stock Exchange. To take an example, we are so far the only country which requires companies to disclose sales and profits divided by different classes of business.

I do not know on what grounds Professor Stamp accuses my institute of 'heavy anti-intellectual bias', for he gives none. But I can assure him he is wrong. The facts are that we want to attract more university graduates, and our efforts are having some success. We are proud to number a prominent academic accountant amongst our council members. We want to see more of our members teaching in universities, and we are actively sponsoring and encouraging research work there and elsewhere.

However, we continue to attach no less importance to practical training and experience than to academic qualification, for the Chartered Accountant has to make decisions based on judgment. Unlike many others, the accountant in practice who makes an error of judgment is liable to have it misinterpreted as professional negligence and to be sued personally for the consequences.

A final word on profit forecasts. In takeover situations I believe it is desirable for directors to give forecasts if they can, otherwise shareholders would be at a disadvantage in trying to judge the value of their shares and the merits of the offer. My institute decided as a matter of policy at the request of the working party of merchant banks engaged in the preparation of the City Code to cooperate in ensuring that such estimates were prepared by directors with proper care and due regard for all relevant information.

While the accountant's part is necessarily restricted to reporting on the calculations and accounting bases—one cannot 'audit' a forecast in the sense in which this word is generally understood—I believe a useful function is performed.

In 1968 there were 140 take-overs of quoted companies involving a total consideration of £1,516,000,000. In how many cases, and by how much in comparison with the total figures involved, did published profit forecasts prove substantially wrong?

(c) Letter to the Editor from Professor Stamp (published 26 September 1969)

Sir,

   I am sorry that Mr. Leach should have received from my article, Auditing the Auditors, the impression that I believe that my objectives are 'immediately achievable' or that I am unaware that the business world is 'highly complex, diverse and volatile'.

   The two points that I was anxious to make were these. First, that this very complexity urgently demands a continuing research programme into accounting principles if accountants and auditors are to live up to their responsibilities; and secondly, that the profession must be seen to be doing this and that auditors must be seen to be independent. In the light of recent events it is clear that protestations of integrity are not enough. Justice must not only be done but be seen to be done.

   I am glad to learn from Mr. Leach of the English Institute's interest in research, which is not immediately apparent on a reading of the Institute's latest annual report where it merits a mere four and a half lines in 39 pages. Certainly I have yet to learn of any concrete evidence of this interest comparable to the $2m. a year which, the American Institute's president has stated, is being spent by the American profession on its Accounting Principles Board.

   Nor do I believe it to be the case that the English Institute has been, or is, in the vanguard where educational standards are concerned. What chance is there that we shall have a graduate accounting profession in England by the early seventies? Yet this is what will be achieved in Canada, a country which Mr. Leach believes is *following* his Institute's lead!

   Finally, I did not, in another article, cite Marks and Spencer as a typical case of British practice, but as an example which the great majority would do well to emulate. It is naughty of the English Institute president not to present a 'true and fair view' of what I said.

                              Yours faithfully,

                                        (s.) Edward Stamp.

Appendix 11

Accountancy **and a 'True and Fair View'**

British accountants have a very heavy commitment to the presentation of a 'true and fair view' of the situations on which they report, and the phrase is one they use frequently in describing their work.

It is therefore noteworthy that in a controversy as important as the one debated between Professor Stamp and Mr. Leach in the columns of *The Times* (*see* Appendix I), *Accountancy* (the official journal of the English Institute, of which Mr. Leach is the president) should choose to present only the one side. They did this by republishing Mr. Leach's *Times* article in their October 1969 issue, after obtaining the permission of *The Times*. Professor Stamp's article in *The Times*, to which Mr. Leach was replying and to which he referred many times, was not republished by *Accountancy*.

This decision was criticised in two letters to the Editor of *Accountancy*, printed in the December 1969 issue (p. 925). Pointing out the importance of the journal maintaining a 'neutral' position in such controversies, they suggested that it would be fairer to readers to publish both sides. One of the letters said it was 'ironical' that the Editor only published one side of a controversy 'partly concerned with the ability of accountants to make independent independent unbiased judgements'. Perhaps *Accountancy* 'could be encouraged to become a forum for serious debate, and not simply a pulpit for authority', if the other side were also printed.

But the Editor refused, and in a waspish little note at the foot of the two letters he said he was sorry that *Accountancy* did not reprint Professor Stamp's article, 'but only because if that had been done I might have been spared the above letters'.(!) Any readers who wished to refer to Professor Stamp's article could, he said, find it in the 11 September issue of *The Times*.

As the Editor of *Accountancy* said, at the end of his little note, 'My trade of journalism (I prefer the word trade to the more pompous term profession) also has its standards'.

Appendix III

Article by Professor Stamp (published in 'The Journal of Business Finance', Vol. 1, No. 1).

The Public Accountant and the Public Interest[1]

The recent proposals for the integration of the accountancy profession in the United Kingdom[2] have drawn attention to the fact that numerically, in relation to accountants employed in industry and Government, the importance of the accountant in public practice is diminishing. A similar trend is evident in North America and in Australasia, and elsewhere. Yet no one would deny that the function of the auditor, in lending credibility to financial statements, has been growing in importance, rapidly and steadily, over the last fifty years. With the growth of the large industrial corporation, entrepreneurs have been unable to supply the required finance from their own resources. This has led to the development of highly sophisticated securities markets in which corporations are able to obtain finance from national—and increasingly from international—communities. Ownership has become divorced from management, and one of the links between the two is the periodic reports on financial condition and progress which are made by managers and directors to shareholders. Such financial reports are relied upon heavily by investors, prospective investors, creditors, security analysts, Governments, and others. The role of the auditor, in lending credibility to these financial statements, is vital in establishing and maintaining confidence in the capital markets. Without such confidence the

---

[1] This paper is based upon the Australian Society of Accountants Endowed Lecture, delivered by the author in the University of Sydney on 30 August 1966.

[2] *See,* for example, *A Scheme for the development of the Accountancy Profession in Great Britain and Ireland* published on 25 July 1968 by The Institute of Chartered Accountants in England and Wales. The Institute estimates (para. 21) that 60 per cent to 70 per cent of its members now enter industry and commerce within three to four years of qualifying.

whole basis of our capitalist system, with its divorce of ownership from management in virtually all major enterprises, would be destroyed.

Thus the continuing importance of the auditor's role is not in dispute. It is a matter of public interest that he should discharge his functions in the most effective manner possible. It is not however the purpose of this article to examine auditors' techniques, which have, on the whole, kept pace with the growth in sophistication of the accounting information systems whose reliability they are designed to investigate. Rather, its purpose is to examine the relationships which exist between the auditor and his client company, the shareholders and directors thereof, and the public at large, and to suggest modifications which seem desirable if the public is to continue to have faith in the role of the auditor.

Before looking at these relationships, however, it is worth considering for a moment the manner in which the auditor 'lends credibility to financial statements' and, in particular, the under-pinnings of financial accounting theory and practice upon which he bases his judgments.

It is generally conceded that it is the responsibility of management to prepare the financial statements which are submitted to shareholders and others.[3] The duty of the auditor is to make such examination of these statements, supporting schedules, and the books and records of the Company, and to obtain whatever other evidence he deems necessary. Having examined and evaluated this evidence, the auditor is then required to express his independent professional and expert opinion as to the truth and fairness of the financial statements. It is this opinion upon which shareholders and other readers of the statements rely when they use the Company's financial statements.

The wording of the standard form of audit report issued in the United States illustrates clearly the frame-work within which the

---

[3] In the United States the Securities and Exchange Commission has stated that 'the fundamental and primary responsibility for the accuracy of information filed with the Commission and disseminated among the investors rests upon management' (4SEC721(1939)). The provisions of Section 148 of the U.K. Companies Act (1948) cover the same essential point although (as is usual in the U.K.) it is the directors upon whom the responsibility is explicitly laid.

auditor must form his opinion. The usual American report reads as follows:[4]

'We have examined the balance sheet of X Company as of June 30, 19— and the related statement(s) of income and retained earnings for the year then ended. Our examination was made in accordance with generally accepted auditing standards, and accordingly included such tests of the accounting records and such other auditing procedures as we considered necessary in the circumstances.

In our opinion, the accompanying balance sheet and statement(s) of income and retained earnings present fairly the financial position of X Company at June 30, 19—, and the results of its operations for the year then ended, in conformity with generally accepted accounting principles applied on a basis consistent with that of the preceding year.'

The standard form of Canadian report is virtually identical. British, Australian, and New Zealand reports differ in several respects, partly as a result of the specific requirements of the Companies Acts (which govern their wording to some degree). In particular the British report states that the Accounts give a 'true and fair view of the state of the Company's affairs' and of its profits for the period under review.

Yet despite the differences in wording, the essential point remains. Whether it is made explicit, as in the American report, or whether it is implied, as in the British report, the auditor judges the fairness of his client's financial statements in relation to a corpus of 'generally accepted accounting principles'.[5]

This phrase is, unfortunately, deceptive. Many of these so called 'principles' are not principles at all but merely descriptions of current or, even worse, past practice; rules which in many cases are drawn up on an *ad hoc* basis to deal with the expediencies of a passing moment. Accounting principles are riddled with inconsistencies and illogicalities and there are so many alternative 'generally accepted' ways of dealing with most accounting problems that it is almost true to say that practically anything is 'true and fair' to some accountant. What masquerades under the title 'generally accepted accounting principles' is a state of chaos. Can any other words describe aptly

---

[4] *Statements on Auditing Procedure No. 33* (New York, American Institute of Certified Public Accountants, 1963) p. 57.

[5] For a closely argued analysis of this proposition, leading to the conclusion that published financial statements do *not* present a 'true and fair view' see W. P. Birkett 'True and Fair—the law and accounting' *The Australian Lawyer* Vol. 7 (1968) pp. 97–115.

APPENDIX III

the situation where, as Chambers pointed out in a recent article, there are over a million combinations of mutually exclusive rules each giving a true and fair view of a Company's state of affairs and its profits?[6] Many of these rules defy even common sense. Thus in writing their report[7] on the collapse of the large Australian Reid Murray Group the two Inspectors, B. L. Murray, Q.C. (now Solicitor General of the State of Victoria) and B. J. Shaw, commented:

'We now say that neither of us is skilled in accountancy and we are aware that much of what we have said will not be accepted by the accounting profession generally. On the other hand we believe that we are accustomed to the use of common sense, and common sense has compelled us to reject a number of the accounting practices used in the Group and, apparently, regarded as acceptable by accountanats.'[8]

The practices to which the Inspectors referred were used in drawing up financial statements which received an unqualified audit report from a major Australian and internationally affiliated accounting firm.

The criticism of 'generally accepted accounting principles' has mounted steadily in recent years and it has not by any means been confined to Australia. An enormous amount of critical material has been published in the United States over the last ten years, and the situation has received unfavourable comment recently in Britain from such quarters as Sir Frank Kearton,[9] and in the comments on the latest G.E.C./A.E.I. accounts (where a substantial portion of the discrepancy between estimated and recorded profits was attributed to 'differences of judgment' over the choice of which accounting principles to use).[10]

---

[6] R. J. Chambers, 'Financial Information and the Securities Markets', *Abacus*, September 1965, p. 16.

[7] *Interim Report of an Investigation under Division 4 of Part VI of the Companies Act 1961 into the affairs of Reid Murray Holdings Ltd. and certain of its Subsidiaries* . . . (Government Printer, Melbourne, 1963). See also, E. Stamp, 'The Reid Murray Affair' *Accountancy*, August 1964, pp. 685–690.

[8] ibid, p. 107.

[9] Sir Frank, Chairman of Courtaulds, stated in June 1968 that he had written to the President of the Institute of Chartered Accountants to complain about the multiplicity of generally accepted accounting principles, and the problems this generates in reconciling pre- and post-acquisition 'principles' in take-overs.

[10] In October 1967, during a 'take-over battle' with G.E.C., A.E.I. forecast profits of £10. million (before tax) for 1967. In July 1968 it became known

It is not my intention to dwell on this situation in the present article. The profession is moving to correct matters, although a final resolution of the problems will not be possible until a coherent body of accounting theory has been developed, and this is many years off at present.[11] The point is that in the meantime an auditor is faced with the fact that in any given company it is possible to 'accept' many different methods of measuring the value of assets, of determining liabilities, measuring income, and hence of drawing up the financial statements of the enterprise. In choosing between these various methods the auditor is required to exercise his professional judgment. Let us consider for a moment the problems to which this gives rise.

In the situation described, where principles are so ill-defined, and where such a large element of judgment is required in interpreting and applying them, the multiplicity of principles (over-lapping, contradictory, and alternative to each other as many are) must make the role of the auditor appear to some as a sinecure. Yet, it is not a sinecure to a professional man of conscience. An auditor is under a good deal of pressure to find a satisfactory 'compromise' when he finds himself in disagreement with a client on matters of 'principle'. There are usually some other public accountants around who will take over if he resigns, or if he is prepared to acquiesce in being fired, as the City of London Real Property Case[12] demonstrated only too vividly. Under such circumstances, if the auditor can find some way of rationalising his client's wishes, some way of accepting his client's choice of 'principle', who will cast the first stone? Indeed with the present lamentable proliferation of acceptable alternatives open to management, one of the few bed-

---

that in fact A.E.I. suffered a loss of £4½ million in 1967. £5. million of the shortfall was attributed to 'matters substantially of fact'. The remaining £9.5 million was attributed to 'adjustments which remain matters substantially of judgment' (adjustments which it is believed related mainly to differences in the 'principles' used in accounting for contracts).

[11] Apart from private research being done in universities, most of the work in this area is being conducted by or under the sponsorship of the American Institute of Certified Public Accountants. See, for example, their *Accounting Research Studies* of which ten have so far been published. Britain is lagging far behind the Americans in accounting research.

[12] For a brief summary of the facts, and the ultimate conclusion see *The Accountant*, 29 June 1963, pp. 842–847, and 13 July 1963, p. 39.

APPENDIX III

rock principles, and it is a highly subjective one, is the moral one of doing what is right. This can lead to the absurd situation where an auditor may find himself taking a stand against what might, in other circumstances, be quite acceptable technically, simply because he questions the probity of the client's motives in deciding to do what has been done. Dr. Johnson said that courage may not be the greatest of the virtues, but it is the one without which all the others are useless. Quite so, but it would be a pity if the courage and integrity of an auditor seemed to be the only defence that shareholders had against the possible depredations of management.

There is another aspect of this situation, and it is one which cannot be lightly disregarded. It is well illustrated by the Reid Murray debacle, where the auditors were very conscious that the group of companies was in a very precarious financial position. The ultimate catastrophe (which eventually occurred) might well have seemed possible if not probable. The auditor's report was a 'clean' one, even though (as the Inspectors suggested) the auditors must have had misgivings. Supposing the misgivings had culminated in a qualified report. The collapse would still have occurred and might indeed have been precipitated, and the argument *post hoc, ergo propter hoc* would then undoubtedly have been raised against the auditors. There can be no doubt that such considerations must weigh heavily in the minds of auditors considering qualifying the accounts of companies in a poor financial situation since it is impossible subsequently to establish that if their judgment had been less harsh the crash would still have taken place.

Such pressures are increased by the fact that, unlike the lawyer, the auditor weighs the evidence and draws his conclusions behind a veil of secrecy. Even the fact that he has had a difference of opinion with his client is not revealed unless his report is qualified. As a result, the auditing profession does not have a body of case law to which an auditor can refer for guidance on contentious issues arising with clients. On the other hand, although this is hardly a mitigating factor, the auditor has the assurance of knowing that unless there is a major collapse, or an investigation, the quality of his judgment is not likely to be reviewed by third parties.

Under such conditions it would be surprising if a form of 'Gresham's Law' did not come into operation, with bad accounting principles driving out the good. Nor is it surprising that there has been pressure from many parts of the financial community in favour of developing and enforcing a set of rigid rules, backed-up by a statutory enforcing agency along the lines of the American Securities and Exchange Commission.

In my view such a cure is likely to be worse than the original disease. It is true that the SEC puts a great deal of authority behind the accountant who insists that SEC requirements must be met. There is no doubt that the independent public accountant needs all the authority that he can get to back up his position. The trouble with an SEC-type solution is that it diminishes flexibility by introducing a set of written rules. If the rules are couched in general terms they will be too vague to be of any real value. On the other hand the more precise and specific they become the less scope there is for an evolutionary adaptation to changing circumstances since the process of changing the rules is likely to be a long and difficult process. Yet it seems likely that the demands for a 'British SEC' will increase unless something is done to improve the present situation. There is however an alternative to the SEC, and it is one that is suggested by, and can be evaluated in the light of, a further consideration of the role and purpose of the auditor.

The essence of the auditor's role and function is to make an expert examination of a company's financial statements, and the evidence supporting them, and to formulate and express an independent judgment of the fairness of such financial statements. His work consists essentially of the process of collection and expert assessment of evidence, combined with an independent judgment of the fairness of the representations made by management to the outside shareholders on the strength of such evidence. Thus it is clear that, in a very important sense, the auditor is a Judge. He reports his judgment to the shareholders, but his judgment is made on statements prepared by management (whose interests may very frequently conflict with those of the shareholders and of third parties who may read and rely upon the financial statements) and the auditor is himself responsible for seeking and collecting the evidence required to support the management's statements. Thus the professional relationship which now exists between the professional accountant and his client is quite different from that which exists between a professional lawyer and his client. This is well brought out in the comments of Lord Denning, made in his dissenting opinion in

APPENDIX III

the *Candler v. Crane, Christmas* case:

> 'There is a great difference between the lawyer and the accountant. The lawyer is never called on to express his personal belief in the truth of his client's case; whereas the accountant who certifies (*sic*) the accounts of his client is always called on to express his personal opinion as to whether the accounts exhibit a true and correct view of his client's affairs; and he is required to do this, not so much for the satisfaction of his own client but more for the guidance of shareholders, investors, revenue authorities, and others who may have to rely on the accounts in serious matters of business.'[13]

The strength of our system of justice and of the fabric of our society depends very heavily on the confidence which the general public places in the judicial system. As I have outlined earlier, it appears that in like manner the confidence of the general investing public in the securities markets, and thus the strength of the capitalist system, depends in large measure on the degree of confidence and trust that shareholders, etc. place in the *judgment* of professional auditors *qua* Judges. One's faith in a Judge however, is based upon certain attributes of his office which are not at present possessed by the professional auditor. Let us examine some of these attributes in more detail.

In the first place the evidence and arguments upon which the Judge forms his opinion are, except in rare cases, heard in open Court. The accountant, by contrast, reaches his decisions behind a cloak of secrecy. In the end he produces a report, but this is a formal document which is seldom qualified so as to give any hint that there might have been any differences of opinion between the auditor and his client's directors on matters of accounting principle. In the accounting profession, which regards 'full disclosure' as such an important principle, it seems odd that the work of the auditor has to be performed in this cloak and dagger atmosphere.

This brings me to a second point. Not only shareholders and investors remain ignorant of what has been discussed and decided. Even more important, the rest of the profession is denied the advantage of perusing the evidence and the decisions, and weighing them in their own minds in the future when deciding similar problems of their own. Similarly, research committees are excluded from access to invaluable material which would greatly aid them in

---

[13] [1951] 1 All ER at page 434.

their attempts to codify a set of 'principles' into some kind of integrated and consistent structure (as is done in the Law). Principles should not be mere descriptions of current practice, but, nevertheless, a real and intimate knowledge of the facts and problems of current practice is invaluable, if not essential, in the process of arriving at a logical and consistent theory of accountancy.

In short, the present procedure makes it impossible for accountants to accumulate a body of precedents similar to those available (and so invaluable) to lawyers in their work. Moreover, the absence of any record of evidence and decisions makes it impossible for thoughtful and disinterested critics to analyse what has been done, with the objective of pointing out ways in which improvements can be made. In a word it inhibits progress. And, by placing a veil around what has been decided and done it may put a premium on mediocrity and incompetence.

A third important difference between the auditor and the Judge lies in the fact that an auditor is employed and paid by his client. This is not so in the case of a Judge, who is not paid by those upon whom he sits in judgment. Is it possible that a Judge in a Court of Law would be regarded as impartial in his judgment if he were? A Judge serves the public interest and it is ultimately the public which gives him his financial independence. It is difficult to accept that the general public would believe its interest was best served by having Judges paid by appellants, or by defendants, or even by counsel.[14]

Another important point of difference lies in the method of appointment. Judges are appointed by the Crown in this country. Political appointments to the Bench are not unknown, particularly in the United States (where Judges are often elected). But in virtually all instances judicial appointments are made in such a way that the public interest is considered. It would be unthinkable today to suggest that a Judge should be appointed by a party to the proceedings, or that he should hold office during such party's pleasure. Auditors, on the other hand, are appointed nominally by one party, the shareholders. In fact, in public companies in particular,

---

[14] An apparent exception is the independent arbitrator who is usually paid by the parties in dispute. Such appointments are, however, of a non-recurring nature and there is no question of the arbitrator's 'security of tenure' being jeopardised by his decision.

it is the other party, the management and directors, to whom the auditor looks for his remuneration and his security of tenure. The public interest is not represented in the process at all.

Several of the above comments reflect somewhat unfavourably on the independence of the position of the auditor, particularly in his relationship to the general public. This situation is made worse when one considers that many auditors are heavily involved in providing services other than that of judging the fairness of the financial statements. Many auditors are also involved as tax advisers, management consultants etc. Such advisory services may cover a very wide range of accounting and business problems, and the quality of the advice given may in many circumstances be revealed, or otherwise, by the form of accounting presentation and disclosure which the client adopts and on which the auditor must pass judgment. Much has been written elsewhere about the impairment of auditors' independence which results. Yet it is naïve to expect that such lucrative management advisory services will be lightly abandoned by the auditing profession. An auditor is in a very favourable strategic position to give such advice. Moreover there is a great deal of value to clients in having their auditors handle such ancillary consulting assignments. There are reciprocal benefits in the conduct of the audit and the consulting work in having one professional firm to do both jobs since knowledge and experience gained in one spills over into the other. Yet although the economics of the situation encourage the development of such 'ancillary services', it is difficult to dispute the fact that their provision by an auditor appears to diminish his independence.

There is another respect in which an auditor is not even required to assume the appearance of independence, at least in British jurisdictions. Thus there is no requirement in the Companies Acts preventing an auditor from holding shares in a client company. Most people might find it difficult to accept that an auditor owning a perhaps substantial investment in the shares of a client company could legitimately be regarded as 'independent'. Such an unfortunate possibility is compounded by the fact that a reader of an auditor's report has no way of knowing whether or not the auditor owns shares in the company upon which he is reporting since he is not required to say!

From all that has been said above it seems clear that it is

difficult to equate the independence of the auditor *qua* Judge with the independence of a Judge in a Court of Law. Not only does the auditor frequently lack the appearance of independence, he sometimes lacks its reality. The traditional answer to such a charge is that it is irrelevant since the really crucial factor is the independence of the auditor's 'state of mind'. Unfortunately it is impossible to make an objective assessment of a state of mind. It can be judged perhaps by the end result of the mental processes, but since this, in the case of an auditor, is his opinion on the client's accounts such as assessment is a question begging operation at best.

It seems clear that people would pay little respect to a judgment in our Courts of Law if the Judge did not have the appearance as well as the reality of complete independence of those whom he has judged. It seems equally clear that the judgment of financial statements ought properly to be done by a person or persons clearly independent of the company, its directors, managers and shareholders.

Consideration of these factors suggests that perhaps the most sensible way of dealing with the problem might be to relieve the auditor of the burden of the judicial function. This would entail the transfer of this function to some other party or parties, and I will deal with this point shortly. For the moment let us examine the auditor's residual role.

I suggest that the auditor should be expected to act the role that is now played by a lawyer representing his client. The auditor would advise his client (the management of the company), and he would represent his client before a Judge or Board which would be truly independent of the client.[15] The auditor, as a professional accountant, would make an examination of the facts, and collect or cause to be collected all the necessary evidence; he would consider and weigh this evidence and form his opinion on the client's financial statements; he would then advise his client as to the proper course to follow in presenting the financial information to the outside world, including the shareholders. The auditor would be employed by the management of the company, *de jure* as well as *de facto,* and he

---

[15] From an operational point of view the 'client' can be defined as 'management'. In the broadest sense this of course includes the directors (although as noted in footnote (3), the practice in the U.S. is to de-emphasise the directors' role).

APPENDIX III

would be responsible for determining, discovering, evaluating and documenting all debatable or contentious matters in much the same fashion as he does under the present system. He would express his opinions and advice to the client and recommend the course to be followed; but he would also be responsible for ensuring that all relevant material pertaining to the accounts was brought to the attention of the Judges, as I shall describe shortly. Whilst he may feel that a certain course should be followed, may recommend it to the client, and the client may adopt it, the auditor would be responsible for seeing that the Judge was fully aware of all aspects of all material contentious or debatable points.

Once the auditor and client had decided their positions the auditor would present to the Judge or Board all necessary details of matters which had to be judged. The auditor, and the client if necessary, would appear before the Judge and give verbal evidence; matters would of course be expedited—as they are now in large accounting firms when two or more partners confer on a client's affairs—by the advance preparation of a detailed memorandum by the auditor explaining the pros and cons of all contentious items for the benefit of the Judge. In fact, submission of such a report by the auditor would be mandatory in all cases, even in cases where no contentious items existed (in which case that fact would be stated). The onus would be on the auditor to make sufficient examination so as to disclose all such items, and to bring all aspects of them before the Judge. It might perhaps be argued that this duty is *too* onerous and that a 'devil's advocate' should be employed by the Judge to dig up any facts which ought to be considered and which have not been brought to light, or brought forward, by the auditor. I must reject this, not merely on the grounds of delay and expense; in my view a professional auditor can be relied upon—*must* be relied upon—to act responsibly and with integrity and to disclose all relevant facts. He must also be relied upon to *discover* all relevant facts.

Nor do I believe that the imposition on him of this responsibility would thereby fail to relieve him of the 'judge function'. The auditor would be responsible for collecting, appraising and presenting evidence. He would also be expected by his client to judge the evidence and render opinions and advice (to the client). But the *Judge* would only require the auditor to present the evidence, facts and opinions; as far as the final judgment is concerned, that would be the responsibility of the Judge alone. While the legal analogy is obvious, it perhaps becomes more so if one makes the comparison with French legal procedure rather than with that customarily used in Anglo-Saxon courts.

Judges, and there would clearly need to be several to deal with the work involved, although they would not necessarily sit together in deciding all issues, would be appointed from the ranks of the most able and experienced members of the profession. The appointment would be for a long term and would be full time and it would be expected to be regarded as the crowning achievement of a man's career in public accounting. The appointment would be made by the profession, not by the government, and Judges' salaries would be paid by the profession out of a fund raised by a levy on all firms audited.[16] The levy would require to be enforced by statute and the basis of the charge would need careful consideration.

The Judge would be empowered to review files, examine witnesses and cross-question the auditors and their clients. Judgments would be published in exactly the same way in which legal judgments are now published. Proceedings would normally be public but judges might hold them *in camera* if they saw fit. Precedents would be established in exactly the same way as is now done in legal practice.

Auditors would represent their client's interests, subject to the proviso that they would have a professional responsibility for ensuring that all material evidence was brought before the Judge. All contentious matters would be decided by the Judge, and if a collapse ensued as a result of disclosures made, no odium would attach to the auditor.

Now I cannot of course attempt to anticipate all of the possible objections which might be raised against my proposal, but one of the potentially most serious is the possibility that implementation of what I have suggested would lead to delays in the submission of accounts to shareholders. Shareholders deserve our sympathy in this matter, and not all of them are especially well served at the present time. The longer the time interval between a company's

---

[16] Alternatively, the fund could be raised by an annual levy imposed and collected by the State. There seems to be no reason why this should introduce a political flavour into the scheme. Indeed, the Judges could be appointed by the Crown on the advice of the profession.

year end and the date a shareholder receives a copy of the Annual Report the more out of date is the Report and the less its value to the shareholder. The auditor is a potential bottleneck since the Annual Report obviously cannot be made available until after the auditor has signed his statement of opinion. Thus the interval between the year end and the date of the auditor's report represents the minimum length of time the shareholder must wait (and they wait several weeks or even months longer in most cases). It is instructive to examine the interval on the case of some major companies. Some illustrations, from different countries, are as follows:

Name of Company, and Year end.		Interval, in days, between Year end and date of auditor's report
Cable Price Downer (New Zealand)	31 March 1968	116
Australian Consolidated Industries	31 March 1968	87
Colonial Sugar Refining (Australia)	31 March 1968	82
Distillers Corporation (U.K.)	31 March 1968	109
Unilever	31 December 1967	82
English Electric	30 December 1967	60

Yet there are other examples which serve to illustrate how much of a 'cushion' there is in present practice. Thus I.B.M., an international corporation with assets in excess of $5.5 billion, has its auditor's report signed 23 days after the year end. Marks and Spencers latest report took only 17 days (and in the previous year, 1967, it took only 14 days). This points out how much slack there is which, if taken up by intelligent use of modern accounting and auditing methods, would provide more time—if this is needed—for implementation of my proposals.

I am not however by any means convinced that what I propose need necessarily involve any further delays in the publication of results. Anyone with experience of the administration of an audit practice knows that a great deal of time is generally and necessarily spent by the senior staff, the managers, and the partners of a firm in discussing tricky and contentious issues and attempting to resolve them. Many of these discussions take place with members of the client's staff. In a well run practice discussion also takes place between partners seeking second, and maybe even third or fourth opinions on the really difficult matters. In the better auditing firms partners' judgments are collective, not individual, and much time is spent in arriving at these judgments because, as I have indicated, it is one of the most onerous responsibilities of an auditor to sit in judgment on his client's statements. If the final judgment had to be made by a third party I can see no reason why the time involved need be any greater. The auditing firm's partners would present the Judge with a memorandum which they would later discuss with him. This would be a discussion between experts and there would be few wasted words. The only really difficult problem might be the scheduling of the Judges' time so as to avoid bottlenecks. This is a relatively simple problem in logistics and need not be regarded as critical.

If necessary, provision in the governing rules of procedure could be made to permit auditors to issue opinions off their own bat subject to later review by the Judge. This would take care of urgent problems where the issues of principle were cut-and-dried and where clear precedents existed. Severe penalties would of course be imposed on anyone who took improper advantage of this procedure. Judges would be armed with powers, similar to those vested in the SEC in the United States, to deal with offenders.

Indeed, one can even contemplate an alternative form of procedure which would certainly avoid delay in all but the most exceptional cases. The profession might establish a judicial procedure similar to that outlined above, arming the Judges with the powers I have described, but with the proviso that Judges would not exercise these powers unless approached voluntarily by a public accountant and asked to act.[17] The onus would then always be on the auditor, in cases where he did not so approach a Judge and where difficulties later appeared, to justify his failure to avail himself of the judicial machinery. Such a scheme would preserve the advantages of the judicial approach while at the same time providing a short-circuit in cases where it was self-evident that it was unnecessary.

Another possible objection is that my proposal will destroy the auditor's independence. But, as I have already pointed out, his independence is eroded beyond repair already in many cases. Nor

---

[17] This is reminiscent of the proposals made by Leonard Spacek. senior partner of the major U.S. firm of Arthur Andersen & Co., in his article 'The need for an Accounting Court', *The Accounting Review,* July 1958, pp. 368–379.

APPENDIX III

is it clear that it is necessary for him to be independent unless he is required to deliver an independent judgment. If the judging function is passed on to a Judge the auditor no longer needs independence. He will of course require competence in his work, and honesty and integrity in his presentation of his client's case and position to the judge—but he needs these qualities now, as does the practising lawyer. It is surely not impossible to conceive of a non-independent auditor retaining his professional honesty and integrity. It might indeed be less difficult for some of the weaker brethren to demonstrate these qualities if my proposals were to be adopted.

Let us now look at the other side of the question, and examine some of the advantages which might be expected to flow from the adoption of the proposals.

In the first place it would liberate the auditor from his present dichotomous role of professional adviser and judge. It will in no way diminish the importance of judgment however; the auditor will still have to exercise all the qualities of professional judgment that he does now, in the examination and assessment of evidence and in the formulation of an expert opinion, and he will be called upon to argue the case for his and his client's opinions and judgments before the Judge. He will also have the heavy responsibility, moral as well as intellectual, of ensuring that all the relevant points, pro and con his own opinion, are brought to the attention of the judge.[18] But he will no longer be placed in the invidious and in many ways ridiculous position of having to judge, publicly, his fee paying client.

This will, I believe, increase, his stature, and that of the profession, in the community, and will silence many of the critics, particularly those who come forward when a crash takes place and when there is an opportunity of shifting some of the blame on to the heads of the auditors.

Secondly, I believe that my system would provide a very effective focus to which ideas and proposals for the reform and development of accounting principles could be directed. There are already bodies and groups which are responsible, within the present organisation of the professional accounting bodies, for work in this area—research committees and foundations etc., to say nothing of the work being done in universities by academics, and their importance would not

---

[18] Such a moral obligation is not unknown in legal practice.

diminish. But the work of the Judges would not merely help in defining and codifying and giving authority to accounting principles, it would implement them. The Judges would not be merely advisers, they would execute decisions. Moreover they would have the responsibility of ensuring that their decisions on accounting principles were not just good decisions in themselves; they would be required to see that they were *consistent* with those being made in other companies and in other parts of the country. Any particular auditing firm may be able to do this now, to some extent and with some of its clients, but there is little co-ordination and consistency between auditing firms on many matters—the fracas in the U.S. recently over the investment credit demonstrated this to those who hadn't realised it long ago.[19]

There may be some tendency on the part of the Judges—and it will have to be controlled—towards conservation and even ossification. It is a tendency to which many older men are prone. But Judge's decisions will be open to criticism, and critics will at least have a central and conspicuous target to fire at rather than the present moving and largely invisible one.

In this way I believe there is reason to hope that my proposal would lead to a rapid increase in the rate at which progress is made in the solution of the dilemmas of principle which now face us.

Thirdly, because the Judge's decision would be published, as legal decisions are now, along with all the evidence (except obviously confidential material) relevant to the decisions, the veils of secrecy which now conceal so much of the sacred cows and rules of thumb of so-called accounting theory, *as it is applied in practice*, would be stripped away. Moreover, the publication of the judgments would promote the making of sound and consistent decisions by auditors and management before bringing them before Judges, since the managers and auditors would have the precedents available. Most important of all, publication of the judgments would make it possible for academics and other thoughtful people to extend the range of their criticism of accounting theory and practice. In fact the scope for analysis and criticism would be increased by an enormous factor. This would have results whose benefits are incalculably great. All of the intellectual resources and analytical abilities of the academic

---

[19] For a brief summary of the issues involved see opinion No. 4 of the Accounting Principles Board (New York, A.I.C.P.A., 1964).

world could be brought to bear on the analysis and criticism of the developing body of decisions and precedents. At the moment all that is available to the academic—in the absence of failure and the consequent Inspector's Report (and even these are seldom produced outside Australia)—are company Annual Reports which, it is no exaggeration to say, conceal more than they disclose in most cases. Even the best Annual Reports tell nothing of the pros and cons that were considered in producing the final product, and many give little clue at all to the accounting 'principles', conventions and rules, actually used in preparing the financial statements, let alone any discussion of the reasons for rejecting alternative courses of action. I am quite sure that an important reason for the slow and uncertain development of accounting theory, compared for example with Medicine and Law, is the fact that whereas there is ample documentation of the facts and the problems of Law and Medicine the practice of accountancy is, by contrast, very poorly documented, and accountants have developed a tradition of secrecy. Under such circumstances it is hardly surprising that the sacred cows and the rules of thumb are reigning supreme throughout much of present day practice.

The implementation of these proposals should be left to the profession. But I do not rule out the possibility that it might be necessary for the Government to act instead, if the profession were unwilling to do so. This could well lead to the establishment of the equivalent of a Securities and Exchange Commission, armed however with more extensive powers than are now exercised by that body. Either way, one could expect a rapid increase in the quality of accounting information presented to shareholders and there is no doubt that such a development is in the public interest. The very high degree of public interest in the quality of the performance of the audit function was emphasised right at the beginning of this article.

If one is realistic, however, one must accept that neither the solution which I have outlined above, nor the introduction of an SEC, is likely to be acceptable to the accounting profession. Let me close by outlining briefly a third possible solution to the problems.

All companies would be required to publish a complete and detailed description of the accounting principles they use in preparing their accounts. Whenever any of these principles or procedures were changed the Company would be required to publish full details of the changes made and the reasons for making them. Either the accounting profession or a specially constituted government agency would maintain a complete record of all of the principles and procedures currently in use, the justification for their use, and the reasons for changes which have been made. This record would become the equivalent of the case law and statute law available to lawyers, and it could be readily maintained and kept up to date on a computer.

Instead of Judges, the profession would establish an Advisory Board whose function would be to advise, and if necessary give rulings, to auditors on any problems relating to accounting principles which might arise in an auditor's practice and which he thought fit to bring to the Board. The onus in all cases would be upon the auditor to decide whether it was necessary for him to approach the Board with a problem, or, having approached the Board, whether he should accept its ruling.

In this way the accounting principles being used by companies would be brought to light and fully disclosed, and there would be the maximum opportunity for the evolution of accounting principles. On the other hand, the increase in the disclosure of what is actually going on behind the scenes in the preparation of company accounts would increase the likelihood of actions being brought against a company, its directors, or its auditors by members of the general public, including shareholders, former shareholders, creditors, etc. However, an auditor faced with such an action need have little to fear provided he had availed himself of the advisory services of the Board. Thus, although auditors would be exposed to greater risks of action, they would be better protected in dealing with an action, provided they could clearly demonstrate that their judgment had had the prior endorsement of the profession.

This solution will not do much to remedy the visible factors which appear to diminish the auditor's independence. But it would do a great deal to speed up the development of accounting principles, and by giving the auditor authoritative support in his interpretation of these principles in contentious areas it should greatly strengthen his independence of mind and outlook. In a sense this solution is a compromise; but a workable compromise is well worth having if it will result in much fuller disclosure of the present state of 'generally

APPENDIX III

accepted accounting principles' and hence in more rapid improvement in the quality of such 'principles'.

The University,
Edinburgh.

February 1969

Appendix IV

The City Code on Take-overs and Mergers[1]

Introduction

The City Code on Take-overs and Mergers first appeared in its present form in March 1968. It was prepared and issued by the City Working Party, a body originally set up in 1959 and reconvened by the Governor of the Bank of England in 1967 for that purpose. On it are now represented the Issuing Houses Association, the Accepting Houses Committee, The Association of Investment Trust Companies, the British Insurance Association, The Committee of London Clearing Bankers, the Confederation of British Industry, the National Association of Pension Funds and The Stock Exchange, London. This new edition incorporates a limited number of revisions and additions made by the City Working Party in the light of experience gained in its operation since that date. Certain of these modifications are the result of suggestions made by the Panel on Take-overs and Mergers established in September 1967 on the proposal of the Governor to supervise the operation of the Code. The Code, nevertheless, both as to its principles and rules, remains substantially in the form in which it was originally issued.

It is generally accepted that the choice before the City in the conduct of Take-overs and Mergers is either a system of voluntary self-discipline based on the Code and administered by the City's own representatives or regulation by law enforced by officials appointed by Government. The City Working Party are firmly of the opinion that the voluntary system is more practicable and more effective.

The provisions of the Code fall into two categories. On the one hand, the Code enunciates general principles of conduct to be observed in bid situations. On the other, it lays down certain rules, some of which are precise, and others no more than examples of

---

[1] Originally published, 27 March 1968. Revised and reprinted, 28 April 1969.

the application of principles. The general principles and these latter rules are of their very nature imprecise.

The City Working Party point out that some of these general principles of the Code, based upon a concept of equity between one shareholder and another, whilst readily understandable in the City may not easily lend themselves to legislation. The City Working Party believe that a code administered by the Panel would possess a degree of flexibility and speed in action which would be difficult to achieve in any more legalistic procedures imposed by statute. They consider also that the reconstituted Panel representative of the City and with its permanent secretariat would be capable of more useful functions before or during the course of a transaction than would be possible if a statutory body were charged with the responsibility of enforcing rigid regulations which would have in the end to be interpreted by the Courts.

Although the Code was drafted with quoted public companies particularly in view, the spirit of the Rules and, except where inappropriate, the letter, should be observed where unquoted public companies are concerned. The Rules and their spirit may also be relevant to transactions in the shares of private companies.

The Panel on Take-overs and Mergers

The Panel referred to in the Introduction is now situated at the Bank of England Building, New Change, London, E.C.4, and communications intended for it should be addressed to The Secretary of the Panel on Take-overs and Mergers at that address.

Attention is drawn to the fact that, in addition to its function as a supervising body in regard to all take-over and merger transactions, the Panel will be available for consultation at any stage before a formal offer is made to a company as well as during the course of a transaction. *Accordingly, in any case of doubt the Panel should be consulted.*

Since, however, it is a matter for a shareholder to decide for himself when and how to dispose of his shares, the Panel cannot be expected to pronounce on the merits or demerits of any individual offer.

Definitions

The Panel means the Panel on Take-overs and Mergers set up at the request of the Bank of England.

Associate. It is not thought practicable to define an 'associate' in precise terms which would cover all the different relationships which may exist in a take-over or merger transaction.

The term 'associate' is intended to cover all parties (whether or not acting in concert with the offeror or offeree company or with one another) who directly or indirectly own or deal in the shares of the offeror or offeree company in a bid situation and who have (in addition to their normal interest as shareholders) an interest or potential interest, whether commercial, financial or personal, in the outcome of the offer.

Without prejudice to the generality of the foregoing the term 'associate' may, on the circumstances of the case, include subsidiary, fellow-subsidiary and parent companies of either the offeror or offeree company; bankers or stockbrokers who normally act for any of the companies concerned and the financial advisers of any of such companies; the Directors (together with their close relatives and related trusts) of the offeror or offeree company or of an 'associate' company; the pension funds of such companies or any pension fund, investment company or unit trust which is accustomed to act on the instructions of any company or individual included in the foregoing description of 'associate'; and any company or individual directly or indirectly holding or acquiring during the course of the bid an interest which (together with any holding it had at the outset of the bid) represents 10 per cent. or more of the equity capital of the offeror or offeree company.

Offer. Offer includes, wherever appropriate, take-over and merger transactions howsoever effected.

Offeror Company. Offeror company includes companies incorporated inside or outside the United Kingdom and individuals wherever resident.

Offer Period. Offer period means the period from the date when an offer is announced until the offer is declared or becomes unconditional or lapses.

Unconditional. References to an offer becoming or being declared unconditional include cases in which the offer has as a result of

APPENDIX IV

the receipt of sufficient acceptances been announced to have become or been declared unconditional subject only to one or more other previously stated conditions including for example the creation of additional capital, the grant of quotation etc. etc., being fulfilled.

General Principles

1. It is considered to be impracticable to devise rules in such detail as to cover all the various circumstances which arise in take-over or merger transactions. *Accordingly, persons engaged in such transactions should be aware that the spirit as well as the precise wording of these general principles and of the ensuing rules must be observed.*

2. While the Boards of an offeror company and of an offeree company and their respective advisers and associates have a primary duty to act in the best interests of their respective shareholders, they must accept that there are limitations in connection with take-over and merger transactions on the manner in which the pursuit of those interests can be carried out. Inevitably therefore these principles and the ensuing Rules will impinge on the freedom of action of Board and persons involved in such transactions.

3. Shareholders shall have in their possession sufficient evidence, facts and opinions upon which an adequate judgement and decision can be reached, and shall have sufficient time to make an assessment and decision. No relevant information shall be withheld from them.

4. At no time after a *bona fide* offer has been communicated to the Board of an offeree company or after it has reasonably come within the contemplation of the Board of an offeree company that a *bona fide* offer is likely to be forthcoming, shall any action be taken by the Board of the offeree company in relation to the affairs of the company, without the approval in general meeting of the shareholders of the offeree company, which could effectively result in any *bona fide* offer being frustrated or in the shareholders of the offeree company being denied an opportunity to decide on its merits.

5. It must be the object of all parties to a take-over or merger transaction to use every endeavour to prevent the creation of a false market in the shares of an offeror or offeree company.

6. A Board which receives an offer or is approached with a view to an offer being made should normally in the interests of its shareholders seek competent outside advice.

7. Rights of control must be exercised in good faith and the oppression of a minority is wholly unacceptable.

8. All shareholders of the same class of an offeree company shall be treated similarly by an offeror company.

9. If, after a bid is reasonably in contemplation, an offer has been made to one or more shareholders of an offeree company, any subsequent general offer made by or on behalf of the same offeror or his associate to the shareholders of the same class shall not be on less favourable terms.

10. During the course of a take-over or merger transaction, or when such is in contemplation, neither the offeror company, the offeree company nor any of their respective advisers shall furnish information to some shareholders which is not made available to all shareholders. This principle shall not apply to the furnishing of information in confidence by an offeree company to a *bona fide* potential offeror company or *vice versa*, nor to the issue of circulars by members of a Stock Exchange to their own investment clients provided such issue shall previously have been approved by the Panel.

11. Directors of an offeror or an offeree company shall always, in advising their shareholders, act only in their capacity as Directors and not have regard to their personal or family shareholdings or their personal relationship with the companies. It is the shareholders' interests taken as a whole which should be considered, together with those of employees and creditors.

12. Any document or advertisement addressed to shareholders containing information, opinions or recommendations from the Board of an offeror or offeree company or its respective advisers shall be treated with the same standards of care as if it were a prospectus within the meaning of the Companies Act 1948. Especial care shall be taken over profit forecasts.

APPENDIX IV

Rules

THE APPROACH

1. The offer should be put forward in the first instance to the Board of the offeree company or to its advisers.

2. If the offer or an approach with a view to an offer being made is not made by a principal, the identity of the principal must be disclosed at the outset.

3. A Board so approached is entitled to be satisfied that the offeror company is or will be in a position to implement the offer in full.

4. Where an offer is being made by a parent company for minority shareholdings of a subsidiary, or in any other case where the offer is not completely at arm's length, it is essential that competent outside advice be obtained in order to ensure, and to satisfy the offerees, that their interests are fully protected.

EARLY STAGES

5. When any firm intention to make an offer is notified to a Board from a serious source (irrespective of whether the Board views the offer favourably or otherwise), shareholders must be informed without delay by Press notice. The Press notice should normally be followed as soon as possible by a circular.

Where there have been approaches which may or may not lead to an offer, the duty of a Board in relation to shareholders is less clearly defined. There are obvious dangers in announcing prematurely an approach which may not lead to an offer. By way of guidance it can be said that an announcement of the facts should be made forthwith as soon as two companies are agreed on the basic terms of an offer and are reasonably confident of a successful outcome of the negotiations.

In any situation which might lead to an offer being made, whether welcome or not, a close watch should be kept on the share market; in the event of any untoward movement in share prices an immediate announcement, accompanied by such comment as may be appropriate, should be made.

6. Joint statements are desirable whenever possible, provided that agreement thereon does not lead to undue delay. The obligation to

make announcements lies no less with the potential offeror company than with the offeree company.

7. The vital importance of absolute secrecy before an announcement must be emphasised.

8. When an offer is announced, the identity of the offeror company must be disclosed and that company must disclose any existing holding in the offeree company which it owns or over which it has control.

BOARD CONSIDERATION OF AN OFFER

9. Directors must always have in mind that they should act in the interests of the shareholders taken as a whole. Shareholders in companies which are effectively controlled by their Directors have to accept that in respect of any offer the attitude of their Board is decisive. Exceptionally, there may be good reasons for such a Board preferring a lower offer or rejecting an offer. Nevertheless, where a Board recommends acceptance of the lower of two offers, or, being a controlling Board, accepts such lower offer or rejects an offer, thus in effect frequently forcing the minority shareholders to act similarly, it must very carefully examine its motive for so doing and be prepared to justify its good faith in the interests of the shareholders as a whole.

10. Directors whose shareholdings, together with those of their families and trusts, effectively control a company, or shareholders in that position who are represented on the Board of a company, and who contemplate transferring control, should not, other than in special circumstances, do so unless the buyer undertakes to extend within a reasonable period of time a comparable offer to the holders of the remaining equity share capital, whether such capital carries voting rights or not. In such special circumstances the Panel must be consulted in advance and its consent obtained.

11. Any information including particulars of shareholders given to a preferred suitor should on request be furnished equally and as promptly to a less welcome but *bona fide* potential offeror. In case of difficulty the Panel must be consulted and its consent obtained.

12. It is essential that after an offer has been announced the offer document and a letter setting out the views of the Board of the offeree company should be circulated as soon as practicable.

If any offeror who has announced his intention to make an offer does not proceed with the formal offer within a reasonable time, he must be prepared to justify the circumstances of the case to the Panel.

FORMAL OFFERS, DOCUMENTS SUPPORTING AN OFFER OR RECOMMENDING THE ACCEPTANCE OR REJECTION OF AN OFFER

13. Any document or advertisement addressed to shareholders under these headings must be treated with the same standards of care with regard to the statements made therein as if it were a prospectus within the meaning of the Companies Act 1948. This applies whether the document or advertisement is issued by the company direct or by an adviser on its behalf. Each document sent to shareholders of the offeree company must state that the Board of the offeror company and/or, where appropriate, of the offeree company (or a Committee of the Board duly authorised by the Board so to act) have considered all statements of fact and opinion contained therein and accept, individually and collectively, responsibility therefore and consider that no material factors or considerations have been omitted.

A copy of the authority from the Board of the company (or the Committee, as the case may be) for the issue of such document must be lodged with the Panel Secretariat.

14. Shareholders must be put into possession of all the facts necessary for the formation of an informed judgement as to the merits or demerits of an offer. Such facts must be accurately and fairly presented and be available to the shareholder early enough to enable him to make a decision in good time. The obligation of the offeror company in these respects towards the shareholders of the offeree company is no less than its obligation towards its own shareholders.

15. Without in any way detracting from the imperative necessity of maintaining the highest standards of accuracy and fair presentation in all communications to shareholders in a take-over or merger transaction, attention is particularly drawn in this connection to profit forecasts and asset valuations.

Notwithstanding the obvious hazard attached to the forecasting of profits, profit forecasts must be compiled with the greatest possible care by the Directors whose sole responsibility they are.

When profit forecasts appear in any document addressed to shareholders in connection with an offer, the assumptions, including the commercial assumptions, upon which the Directors have based their profit forecasts, must be stated in the document.

The accounting bases and calculations for the forecasts must be examined and reported on by the auditors or consultant accountants. Any Merchant Bank or other adviser mentioned in the document must also report on the forecasts. The accountants' report and, if there is an adviser, his report, must be contained in such document and be accompanied by a statement that the accountants and, where relevant, the adviser, have given and not withdrawn their consent to publication.

Wherever profit forecasts appear in relation to a period in which trading has already commenced, the latest unaudited profit figures which are available in respect of the expired portion of that trading period together with comparable figures for the preceding year must be stated. Alternatively, if no figures are available, that fact must be stated.

When revaluations of assets are given in connection with an offer the Board should be supported by the opinion of independent professional experts and the basis of valuation clearly stated.

16. The offer document must state the shareholdings of the offeror company in the offeree company together with the total of the shareholdings in the offeree company in which Directors of the offeror company are interested. The document of the offeree company advising its shareholders on an offer (whether recommending acceptance or rejection of the offer) must (*a*) detail the shareholdings of (i) the Directors of the offeree company in the offeree company and the offeror company and (ii) the offeree company in the offeror company and (*b*) inform shareholders whether the Directors of the offeree company intend, in respect of their own beneficial shareholdings, to accept or reject the offer. If any such shareholdings referred to in this Rule have been purchased within six months of the date of the offer document, the details,

APPENDIX IV

including dates and costs, must be stated. If no such purchases have been made, this fact must be stated.

17. Where the offer is for cash or includes an element of cash, the offer document must include confirmation by the adviser or by another appropriate independent party that resources are available to the offeror company sufficient to satisfy full acceptance of the offer.

18. Documents sent to shareholders of the offeree company recommending or rejecting offers must contain particulars of all service contracts in force for Directors with the offeree company or any of its subsidiaries which have more than twelve months to run and, if entered into within six months of the date of the document, the dates of the contracts and particulars of any immediately preceding contracts. Offer documents on behalf of the offeror company should state whether its Directors' emoluments will be affected by the acquisition of the offeree company.

19. In order to facilitate the work of the Panel, copies of all public announcements made and all documents bearing on a take-over or merger transaction must be lodged with the Panel Secretariat at the same time as they are made or despatched.

MECHANICS OF THE FORMAL OFFER

20. No offer for the whole of the equity share capital of a company (or for a proportion of such equity capital which, if accepted in full, would result in the offeror company having voting control of the equity share capital of the offeree company) shall be made unless it is a condition of such offer that the offer will not become or be declared unconditional unless the offeror company has acquired or agreed to acquire (either pursuant to the offer or by shares acquired or agreed to be acquired before or during the offer) by the close of the offer shares carrying over 50 per cent. of the voting rights attributable to the equity share capital. Accordingly no such offer shall become or be declared unconditional unless the offeror company has acquired or agreed to acquire more than the said 50 per cent.

21. An offer must initially be open for at least twenty-one days after the posting of the offer and, if revised, it must be kept open for at least eight days from the date of posting written notification

of the revision to shareholders: an acceptor shall be entitled to withdraw his acceptance in any case after the expiry of twenty-one days from the first closing date of the initial offer, if the offer has not by such expiry become or been declared unconditional; such entitlement to withdraw shall be exercisable until such time as the offer becomes or is declared unconditional.

No offer (whether revised or not) shall be capable of becoming or being declared unconditional after the expiration of 60 days from the date the offer is initially posted, nor of being kept open after the expiry of such period unless it has previously become or been declared unconditional.

Other than in the circumstances that a competing offer has been declared or has become unconditional, a formal offer may not be withdrawn during its currency except with the permission of the Panel. An offer which is allowed to lapse because of the non-fulfilment of a condition is not to be treated as withdrawn for the purpose of this Rule.

22. After an offer has become or is declared unconditional, the offer must remain open for acceptance for not less than fourteen days, except in the event that the offer becomes or is declared unconditional on an expiry date and the offeror company has given at least ten days' notice in writing to the shareholders of the offeree company that the offer will not be open for acceptance beyond that date.

If in accordance with the provisions of Rule 24 an unconditional declaration becomes void and is subsequently reinstated, the period of fourteen days above referred to will run from the date of the second declaration.

23. An offeror company which has extended an offer must announce the fact not later than 9.30 a.m. on the working day next following the day on which the offer would otherwise have expired.

24. By 9.30 a.m. at the latest on the working day next following the expiry of the first offer, or of any extended or revised offer, whichever may be the later (the relevant day), the offeror company shall announce and simultaneously inform the Stock Exchange:—

    (a) either that the offer has become or is declared unconditional or that the offer has been allowed to lapse, and in the first event,

(b) the total number of shares (as nearly as practicable) (i) for which acceptances of the offer have been received (ii) held before the offer period and (iii) acquired or agreed to be acquired during the offer period.

If the offeror company is unable within the above time limit to comply with any of these requirements, the Stock Exchange will consider the suspension of dealings in the offeree company's shares and, where appropriate, in the offeror company's shares until the relevant information is given. If the offeror company, having declared an offer unconditional, fails by 3.30 p.m. on the relevant day to comply with any of the requirement of sub-para (b) of this Rule, its unconditional declaration shall be void. Immediately thereafter and until the offer is again declared unconditional any acceptor shall be entitled to withdraw his acceptance. Subject to the provisions of the second paragraph of Rule 21, the offeror company may again declare the offer unconditional after it has satisfied the requirements of sub-para (b) of this Rule but not before the expiry of eight days after the relevant day.

25. The obligations of the offeror company and the rights of the offeree company shareholders under Rules 20–24 must be specifically incorporated in the offer document.

26. Generally speaking bids for less than 100 per cent. of the equity capital of an offeree company not already owned by the offeror company or any of its subsidiaries are undesirable. If there are circumstances in which a general offer for less than 100 per cent. is in the opinion of the offeror company justified, it must be made to all shareholders of the class and arrangements must be made for those shareholders who wish to do so to accept in full for the relevant percentage of their holdings. Other than in special circumstances (in which case the consent of the Panel must be obtained) no partial bid may be made to which Rule 20 would not apply. A partial bid to which Rule 20 is not applicable may not be declared unconditional unless acceptances are received for the number of shares bid for.

It is recognised that there may be very exceptional circumstances where in the interests of all the shareholders a deal might be made with a significant minority without a similar offer being made to the other shareholders. In such circumstances the Panel must be consulted in advance and its consent obtained.

27. Where an offer is made for more than one class of share, separate offers must be made for each class and the offeror company should state that it will resort to compulsory acquisition powers under Section 209 of the Companies Act 1948, only in respect of each class separately.

28. When an offer is made for equity capital and there are convertible securities outstanding, arrangements must be made to offer to the holders of such securities such amendment of the conversion terms or other appropriate arrangements as to ensure that their interests are not prejudiced. Where options or subscription rights are outstanding this Rule also applies *mutatis mutandis*.

DEALINGS

29. Save in so far as appears from this Code, it is considered undesirable to fetter the market. Accordingly, all parties to a take-over or merger transaction (other than to a partial bid) and their associates are free to deal at arm's length subject to daily disclosure to The Stock Exchange, the Panel and the Press (not later than 12 noon on the dealing day following the date of the relative transaction) of the total of all shares of any offeror company or the offeree company acquired or sold by them or their respective associates for their own account on any day during the offer period in the market or otherwise and at what average price.

In addition all purchases and sales of shares of any offeror or the offeree company made by associates for account of investment clients who are not themselves associates must be similarly reported to The Stock Exchange and to the Panel, but need not be disclosed to the Press.

In the case of a partial bid the offeror company and its associates may not deal in shares of the offeree company during the offer period for their own account, nor in the case of a partial bid to which company for their own account during a period of twelve months beginning on the last day of the offer period.

APPENDIX IV

30. No dealings of any kind (including option business) in the shares of the offeror and offeree companies by any person who is privy to the preliminary take-over or merger discussions or to an intention to make an offer may take place between the time (*a*) when the initial approach is made or intimated or (*b*) when there is reason to suppose that an approach or an offer will be made and the announcement of the approach or offer or of the termination of the discussions as the case may be.

31. If the offeror company alone or in association with others purchases shares in the market or otherwise during the offer period at above the offer price (being, in the event of the terms of an original offer being revised, the final bid price under the revised terms of an offer) then it shall offer an increased price to all acceptors, such price being not less than the weighted average price (excluding stamp duty and commission) of the shares so acquired during the offer period. If the offer involves a further issue of already quoted securities, the value of such securities shall normally be calculated for the purpose of ascertaining what increased price shall be paid (but not for the purpose of establishing whether any purchase was made at a price above the offer price) by reference to the average of the mean of the daily quotation (as stated in the Stock Exchange official list) of the securities during the offer period. If the offeror company considers that the terms of the previous sentence should not apply to an offer (if, for instance, it considers there has been a general change in market prices during the offer period or facts have been published causing a change in the market value of the securities of the offeror company) the offeror company should consult the Panel. If the offer involves the issue of securities which are not already quoted the value shall be based on a reasonable estimate of what the opening price might be.

32. Since arrangements to deal, purchases and sales with special conditions attached are not capable in every circumstance of being extended to all shareholders, such arrangements to deal, purchases and sales whether during, or in anticipation of, a bid must not be made.

33. Since dealings in the market or otherwise by an associate of an offeror or offeree company may result in a *bona fide* offer being frustrated or may affect the outcome of a bid, such associate is

advised to consult the Panel in advance and where he has not done so must be prepared to satisfy the Panel that his action was not prejudicial to the interests of shareholders generally of the offeror or the offeree company as the case may be.

CHANGES IN THE SITUATION OF A COMPANY DURING A BID

34. During the course of an offer, or even before the date of the offer if the Board of the offeree company has reason to believe that a *bona fide* offer is imminent, the Board must not, except in pursuance of a contract entered into earlier, without the approval of the shareholders in general meeting, issue any authorised but unissued shares, create or issue or permit the creation or issue of any securities carrying rights of conversion into or subscription for shares of the company, or sell, dispose of or acquire or agree to sell, dispose of or acquire assets of material amount or enter into contracts otherwise than in the ordinary course of business. Where it is felt that an obligation or other special circumstance exists, although a formal contract has not been entered into, the Panel must be consulted and its consent obtained.

REGISTRATION OF TRANSFERS

35. The Board and officials of an offeree company should take action to ensure during a take-over or merger transaction the prompt registration of transfers so that shareholders can freely exercise their voting and other rights. Provisions in Articles of Association which lay down a qualifying period after registration during which the registered holder cannot exercise his vote are highly undesirable.